THE
NEW WINES OF
SPAIN

THE
NEW WINES OF
SPAIN
TONY LORD

CHRISTOPHER HELM
London

THE WINE APPRECIATION GUILD
San Francisco

© 1988 Tony Lord
Christopher Helm (Publishers) Ltd, Imperial House,
21–25 North Street, Bromley, Kent BR1 1SD

British Library Cataloguing in Publication Data

Lord, Tony
    The new wines of Spain.
    1. Wine and wine making—Spain
    I. Title
    641.2′2′0946   TP559S8

    ISBN 0-7470-2002-7

Published in the United States by:
THE WINE APPRECIATION GUILD
155 Connecticut St.
San Francisco, CA 94107

    ISBN 0-932664-59-8

Library of Congress No. 88-50080

Typeset by Cotswold Typesetting Ltd, Gloucester
Printed and bound by Butler and Tanner Ltd, Frome, Somerset, England

CONTENTS

ACKNOWLEDGEMENTS

To Hazel and Wendy, two lovely ladies

The author would like to thank all the members of the Spanish wine industry who took the time and trouble to discuss their wines and their country. Particular thanks to Jeremy Watson, David Balls and Maria José Taylor of Wines From Spain, and Graham Hines and Bryan Buckingham of the Sherry Institute, who provided the photographs and much information for the book, and made the many enjoyable trips to Spain possible.

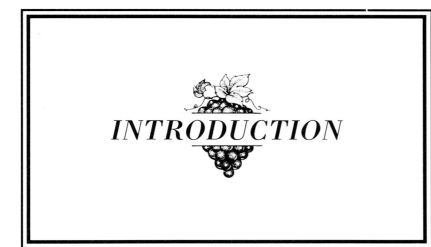

INTRODUCTION

Spain is a remarkably sophisticated country, despite the efforts of some of its citizens to have us believe otherwise. The elegance and charm of Madrid or Barcelona are a far cry from the hideous vulgarity of the modern package holiday resorts, which apart from the sun have little or nothing to do with the real Spain.

It could hardly be otherwise. Long before the great cities and cultures of northern Europe came into being, Spain was a centre of civilisation in western Europe through the learned influence of the Moors. And after their departure, Spain remained a great and powerful kingdom, one of the greatest in the world. It produced El Greco, Goya and Velazquez, men like Pizarro and Cortez who conquered half the Americas, and, as one of the country's greatest admirers in modern times, Sacheverell Sitwell, wrote, the greatest builders since the Romans. 'The Spanish cathedrals, and not only Toledo, Seville, Burgos, Compostella, but a host of lesser ones, are unparalleled, not for the stone vessels alone, but for the extraordinary nature and richness of their contents', he added.

Part of the Spanish culture, one of its civilising influences, has always been wine, and today Spain's 1.6 million hectares of vines represent 16 per cent of the world's total.

Grape vines came to Spanish shores with the wandering Phoenicians and Greeks, and even during the centuries of Moorish occupation, the art of viticulture flourished. Even the Islamic conquerors found ways around their own laws to enjoy Spanish wine.

Sadly though, the Spanish viticulturalists of the twentieth century, if you could call them that, almost destroyed this proud and ancient heritage, a history of making wines that won high praise from those who travelled the land in earlier times. Spain became equated, and almost shackled, with an image of a country dedicated to the art of making rough red wine to be consumed by the colourful peasant at the rate of a litre a day, and by the less colourful tourist looking for a cheap holiday in the sun.

The Rioja went quietly on its way, making sophisticated red wines and some superb whites, for the handful of Spanish *aficionados* who knew about them, while the Jerezanos quietly plied their historic trade in fine sherries. Elsewhere it was a land of vinous chaos. Millions upon millions of litres of rough red wine and unpalatable, often oxidised, white wine flooded into the local bars, or were shipped to other countries where the poor but thirsty generation of the Swinging Sixties were discovering the taste of wine, unfortunately from the bottom up. Little wonder that the major wine buyers of the day saw Spain only as a source of cheap plonk.

For a handful of younger winemakers, the new crusaders, it was not good enough. Past history and present research showed there was absolutely no reason why the climate and soils of Spain could not yield noble wines, and grafting modern winemaking techniques onto their native land, they set about doing so.

Most likely their efforts would have gone largely unrecognised. Their wines would have remained idle curiosities, to be remarked upon and written about, though not truly representative of Spain. But a more persuasive force was at work—the consumer.

Spain has a recent history of producing wine in excess of its own needs, yet the younger generation of the country, the more cosmopolitan citizens of the big cities, were not in the market for cheap wine. If they were going to drink Spanish wine, it had to be good wine. The rough red of their fathers did not suit their palates or their image. Father may still drink it, and in many rural parts of the country still does, but they would not.

Other countries would not take it either. Some had their own wine lakes, in others the new wine drinker was growing too sophisticated in taste to absorb the Spanish lake.

To survive, the Spanish winemaking industry had to change. And change it did. Into the industry came the dual catalysts of modern winemaking and modern marketing. They swept aside the old notion that all a winery had to do was make wine, then foist it on a captive audience.

The Spanish wine industry today is one largely dominated by the co-operatives, and they, by and large, have been forced to alter their thinking, both by the market and by the government, which has been one of the most progressive in western Europe, pushing its wine industry into the modern world through a system of tight restrictions and controls, and enlightened support of those seeking to go forward. Some co-operatives are now even competing on equal terms with the private producers, but it is those producers who have done most to enliven and advance Spanish viticulture and oenology.

It is private money that has led the latter-day Renaissance, even in the most unlikely areas such as the dust bowl of La Mancha, home of the Spanish wine lake. When the private producer shows that an area can yield good wines that will sell at a premium price, the co-operative grower might just get the message that if he adapts, he could make more money for himself. If he doesn't he could be out of business.

Such private producers are dotted here, there and everywhere in Spain. Twenty years ago, few of them existed. Their colleagues owe them a great debt of gratitude, for they have provoked international interest in Spanish wines, and a revival of domestic pride in them, that has saved the industry from the vinous scrap heap.

Some have gone in one direction, basing their hopes for the future on the introduction of noble varieties from other countries. A handful are making varietal wines from these grapes, wines that have excited several leading American palates. But the more sensible are using them to enhance wines made from native Spanish varieties, to give those wines an added dimension, rather than compete with similar wines from other countries that have been making them far longer.

Other producers have gone in a different direction, back to their roots. They are concentrating on how to get the very best out of what they already have, how modern ways can help them improve the wines of their forefathers.

These progressive producers have been successful in both directions, and Spain can now be proud that it has wines that can stand up and be counted while remaining distinctively Spanish. The New World countries, led by Australia, California and New Zealand, are showing that the Old World has no stranglehold on the production of fine wines, and are pressing hard on the heels of the wine world's leader, France. So it is in Spain's best interests to remain Spain, and let the individualistic flavours of its own wines find their own appreciative audience in a world where imitation rather than individualism is narrowing the consumer's choice of wine flavours.

Spain's recent entry into the European Economic Community will help its wine industry. Not only will it give Spain better access to those non-wine-producing members of the community, but it is already bringing agricultural aid funds into the country to help those wineries ready and willing to try to lift their wine quality higher, while curbing and restricting those that will not.

Spain still produces a lot of indifferent wine. But then so does France, Germany, Italy and California, to name but a few. The old image of the colourful peasant grower, with his black beret and three-day, non-designer stubble, is fading fast.

The Spanish themselves, a proud race and intensely insular in both senses of the word, which is to their credit, will not be drinking the wines of France or Italy since EEC entry. They will stay with the wines of Spain. They have such a marvellous gastronomic tradition, with some of the best restaurants in the world serving some of the simplest, most distinctive yet pleasurable foods. It is only fitting that in the new wave wines of Spain they have wines to complement their own, home-grown culinary art once again.

CHAPTER 1

The Wine Laws

At various times throughout the history of the Spanish wine industry, laws have been passed and decrees proclaimed to protect its better wines, usually to counter unscrupulous wine traders adulterating those wines with cheaper imports to make a fast peseta. For example in 1102, after pleas from its producers, King Sancho of Navarra gave protection to the wines of the Rioja, and through the centuries similar protection was given to wines from other regions.

However, the modern Spanish wine laws did not really have their birth until around the beginning of the century when it became apparent that Spain would have to look after the reputation of its better wines not only within Spain, but also in its export markets.

Guidelines for countries introducing an appellation system had already been drawn up at a series of international conferences, and the Spanish authorities used these guidelines to draw up its system of *Denominaciones de Origen* for those areas producing 'wine or spirits of wine with an established name and corresponding repute'. It was decided that each denominacion would be administered by a local Consejo Regulador, comprised of local experts who would draw up their own rules and regulations based on their local knowledge and experience, though within an overall framework of international acceptability.

The first Consejo was created for the Rioja region in 1926, to be followed by Jerez in 1933, Malaga in 1937, Montilla in 1944, and right up to the newest denominacion, that for Toro, which came into being in June 1987, a pace behind other new denominacions like Somontano and Terra Alta. Spain now has 30 denominaciones, including the provisional one for Cava wines, the only one not to be geographically based.

Each denominacion has its rules laid down in a Regulamento, and there are stiff penalties for any producer found going against its rules. Watching over the whole system is the Madrid-based Instituto Nacional de Denominaciones de Origen [INDO].

Each Regulamento may vary slightly to take into account local conditions, but basically it will cover the following areas: where vines may be planted, which vines may be planted, how many vines can be planted per hectare, how they should be trained and pruned, and rules covering unhealthy grapes.

Maximum yields per hectare are laid down, and in the winery there are rules governing the use of standard additives such as sulphur dioxide, used to prevent oxidation. Minimum periods for ageing quality wines are laid down, as are regulations covering what a producer can and cannot say on his label.

Wines labelled this and that, particularly those destined for export, must pass through a series of taste and chemical analysis checks in the laboratories of the respective Consejos to be issued with the Consejo seal of authenticity. Each Consejo has developed its own distinctive seal, and each seal is numbered, so if there are any complaints the Consejo can trace its origins right back to the vineyard where it was born. For example, if a customer complained that a wine purporting to be a Rioja gran reserva, which should have spent two years at least in oak, showed absolutely no oaky flavours, its history can be traced to verify its authenticity by obtaining the number on the seal of guarantee.

In general, the Consejo system works pretty well. Some of the lesser known ones could improve their regulation a little, and stop letting through wines that really do not typify what the area is producing. But it is hard to tell a local winemaker who may be a friend, or even a relative, that he is making poor wine and is not going to get the seal of authenticity and be allowed to call his wine Rioja or sherry. It would destroy his livelihood. But then this doesn't happen in Spain alone.

The Spanish system also works well because it has an inbuilt flexibility. So for example in the Penedes or Navarra the Regulamento has been amended to allow the planting of imported noble grape varieties like Chardonnay or Cabernet Sauvignon, once trials have shown that the use of these varieties can enhance the quality of the wine of the region. The producers in Spain enjoy more freedom than their Italian counterparts. Some of the greatest wines of Italy have to call themselves table wine, the lowest possible indication of quality, simply because they are made from grape varieties not permitted under local rules, and those rules are inflexible.

Equally it is hoped the Spanish authorities will not succumb to another Italian malaise. Already there are two or three Spanish denominaciones that produce so little bottled wine that they really should not have been accorded the honour. And there are other Spanish regions jockeying for denominacion.

The Italian system of appellation has been virtually destroyed as a credible system by the authorities bending to political pressure to grant appellation to almost any area where votes will be lost if they don't. The Spanish must not let themselves suffer the same fate.

No appellation system is perfect, but the Spanish system is reasonably well run, and the industry has not been beset by the recent wine scandals that rocked Italy and Austria, and even led to prosecutions in Germany, where the authorities are meticulous.

So that sticker on the back of the best bottles of Spanish wine means the consumer is getting what he pays for.

CHAPTER 2

Rioja

If one approaches the Rioja region from the west, from Bilbao, the old road twists and turns up the valley of the Iregua. This is Basque country, a land of high, forested mountains and meadows, split by narrow gorges carved by rivers feeding on the melting snows of the high Pyrenees.

The old road eventually reaches the Puerto de Piqueras, some 1700 metres above sea level, then begins the descent, alongside the rushing Ebro river, into the mountain-ringed valley that is the easterly part of the Rioja.

If one comes from the opposite direction, from Barcelona, the country is dramatically different. Semi-arid with dark red-brown soils, bare earth to which stunted bushes cling, including wild thyme, providing meagre fodder for scrawny sheep, this part of the Rioja has been carved by wind erosion into a series of mesas and small valleys of quite desolate appearance.

Together these dissimilar stretches of Spain make up the delimited Rioja region, home of the country's flagship red wines.

The western part of the Rioja, at least, was a wine growing area long before its conquest by the Romans, and there is evidence that they increased its production. With the Moorish conquest of 711 AD, winemaking ceased until the reconquest by the Catholic kings.

In the Mediaeval period, the old pilgrim trail to Santiago de Compostella wound through the western Rioja, and pilgrims must have welcomed the sight of such monasteries as Santo Domingo de la Calzada, now a government-owned Parador hotel, after a hard trek across the mountains. They helped spread the reputation of Rioja wines, though at that time the region was producing far more white wine than red. The change was to come later, in the 1800s.

France, or Bordeaux to be precise, exerted a seminal influence on the modern development of the Rioja, on three separate occasions. When oidium, a leaf mould, severely damaged the Bordeaux vineyards in the 1850s, with a consequent loss of production, the Bordeaux negociants turned to the Rioja for strong red wines to bolster their skinny clarets.

The same negociants, and this time the vineyard owners as well, turned to the Rioja when the far more serious phylloxera louse, a bug that attacks and kills the vine roots, destroyed thousands upon thousands of hectares of the Bordeaux vineyards from the 1870s onwards. Many of them moved, lock, stock and barrel to the Rioja, to begin again.

Much has been made of the French influence on the Rioja and the way its wines are made, dating from this period, particularly on vinification techniques and the use of barrels to mature the wine. However, I am pretty certain these changes would have come anyway. The French presence merely forced the issue.

Many of the Bordelais returned home when it was discovered their old vineyards could be protected from phylloxera by grafting the vines onto resistant American rootstocks, and others left when they found the louse had followed them to the Rioja to repeat its destructive work between 1900 and 1905. However, a good few remained, helping to shape the way Rioja wines were made, until the outbreak of the Spanish Civil War made it unwise for them to stay. This, and the two World Wars, severely disrupted the trade in Rioja wines, and it is fair to say that the Rioja fell back into virtual anonymity.

Again it was what happened in Bordeaux that changed the life of the Riojans yet once more. Fuelled by a wave of speculative interest in clarets, largely emanating from the United States, opening prices for the 1970 clarets surged ahead to new highs. The upward spiral continued with the 1971 vintage, then reached ridiculous levels for the inferior 1972 vintage. As a result the traditional buyers, particularly the British, found themselves financially frozen out of the claret market. They could not, or would not, pay prices that when translated to the bottle on the shop shelf would deter all but the most ardent admirers of fine claret.

At that point, Rioja red wines were well nigh unknown. Connoisseurs in other parts of Spain were drinking them, and a handful of aficionados in other countries than Spanish-influenced parts of the world, where most exports went. It was the British, and later other buyers, casting round for something to replace their unaffordable day-to-day clarets, who rediscovered the Rioja reds.

It has been repeatedly said that in those reds the buyers found something quite akin to decent clarets. I have not found this so. Any regular wine drinker familiar with claret and Rioja red wine should, if the wines were served blind, be able to spot the difference with relative ease. It is only the handful of red Riojas that are made with more than a nod to Bordeaux that could cause any doubt.

More likely the attraction to the British and other buyers of the Rioja was that here they could find good quality red wines, a new discovery to titillate their customers, at remarkably inexpensive prices. And discoveries they were. The encyclopaedic Hugh Johnson, writing at about this time for his book *Wine*, published in 1974, praises the wines of five bodegas, and says he has come across good wine from half a dozen more. A decade later, in *Wine Companion*, his selection of leading world wineries, over thirty Rioja bodegas rate a mention.

At the point of its rediscovery in the early 1970s, the Rioja wine industry had changed little since the arrival of the first Frenchmen a century before. Difficult to reach due to the encircling Sierra Cantabrica, with little or nothing to attract even the most adventurous tourist, it remained a sheltered part of Spain.

The tiny patchwork vineyards, a legacy of centuries of splitting through inheritance under the Napoleonic code, were worked by hand by sturdy peasant farmers who grew grapes to provide them with their own wine and some cash from the grapes they sold on. Cereals, potatoes, tomatoes, small patches of grazing land for a few cows or sheep, jostled the vineyards.

The existing wineries depended on this near feudal system of agriculture for their grapes, as few owned any vineyards at all. Modern viticulture and vinification techniques were all but unknown. The arrival of the foreign buyers was to bring about a profound change to the Riojan wine industry.

As demand began to outstrip supply, the existing bodegas

The best Rioja wines have a hand-made wire mesh around the bottle, originally to stop barmen replacing the wine with something inferior.

began to make very nice profits indeed, despite the fact that they were probably selling their wines at undervalued prices. And profits have a way of attracting outsiders. Before long other Spanish companies, some in the wine business, others not, began to move in, followed by rivals from outside Spain. These new boys knew all about modern vinification, and soon existing wineries were being thoroughly modernised, and a wave of new

7

ones built. Visitors to the cellars of Paternina, Faustino Martinez, Marques de Caceres, Domecq, Berberana, Lan, Lagunilla, Montecillo, Navajas, El Coto, Martinez Bujanda, the superb Olarra cellars, the new Franco-Espanolas complex or Gomez Cruzado, to name but a few, are seeing cellars that did not exist a quarter of a century ago.

A handful of bodegas have resisted introducing all but the most necessary modern vinification techniques, but by and large the old open concrete or large old oak vat fermenters have been replaced by serried ranks of temperature controlled stainless steel fermenters, modern laboratories monitor the progress of the wine through its various stages, small new oak barrels are used to mature the wine instead of aged casks, automatic sterile bottling has largely replaced hand bottling, and statutory controls are in force to ensure Rioja wines are of a proper quality.

In the vineyards, the peasant farmer still tends his grapes, but he is more likely to be driving a tractor than walking behind a mule, and in a move led by Domecq, the bigger bodegas are now tending to plant their own vineyards on a scale that can include mechanical harvesting and the proper use of pesticides to give healthy grapes. Picking at the best time to get the proper balance of sugar and acidity has become the norm, rather than waiting for the highest level of potential alcohol. And weather patterns and soil compatibility with the different grape varieties have both come under increasing scrutiny. In short, in terms of winemaking, the Rioja is now firmly in the twentieth century.

The boom of the middle to late 1970s has now stabilised, but the prosperity it has brought to the region has changed it. Logrono, the provincial capital, is a bustling town of banks and high rise apartments, and the young are moving off the land to work in more rewarding, less arduous jobs. The town now has three or four hotels of a very decent standard, and one restaurant that would be worth a star in any Michelin guide. The need to move wine has even led to the recent completion of a new autoroute through the region.

Yet apart from the questing vinophile, the Rioja remains well off the tourist trail, which in one way is a pity, in another a blessing. For it is a very pretty part of Spain, and outside Logrono it seems time has stood still. The steely grey Sierra Cantabrica mountains provide a dramatic backdrop to the rolling landscape, split by the Ebro River and its tributaries, among them the Rio Ojo, the contraction of which gave the name Rioja. On the highest hills are the old fortified towns, built to protect the locals

Modern bottling lines ensure wines are stable and free from contamination.

from the Moors. Briones is typical. Approached only by a single twisting road, it has sheer drops to the valley floor on three sides, with sweeping views, and sturdy doors that once locked must have left the most determined invader with little hope except siege by starvation.

This is typical Rioja Alta and Alavesa country, two of the three subdivisions of the region. The smaller Alavesa region lies to the north of the Rio Ebro, the larger Alta to the south—despite its name, it is not higher in altitude. The third region, Rioja Baja, is the largest and lies to the east, towards Barcelona. As far as vines go, and almost anything else for that matter, it is the least cultivated in terms of size, but has more vines than Alavesa.

Despite being part of the whole, each region is different in its own way. Administratively, there is the curious distinction that Rioja Alavesa is in control of the Basque government while Alta and Baja are looked after by the regional council. As a result, a lot of money has been spent on promoting Alavesa wines, which are trumpeted as the best, and not much on the other two regions' wines. There have even been moves to distance Alavesa from the other two, to try to distinguish its wines from Rioja per se. But as so much blending goes on between the three regions' wines, this exercise seems rather futile. If a producer proclaims his wine is Alavesa wine, he is doing so because he is proud of it.

The more important distinction is geographical—the way in which the differing climates and soils manifest themselves in the flavour of the wine. The Alavesa is the highest, coolest area, with mainly limestone and clay soils. Its red wines are deep in colour, well perfumed, with good fruit flavours but low acidity levels. The slightly warmer Rioja Alta has two soil types, a different type of clay to the Alavesa with a high iron content, and alluvial river soils. Its red wines have a little less depth of colour, less aroma, a bit less body, but more acidity than the Alavesas, and will keep longer.

These two regions have an Atlantic climate, while the Rioja Baja is distinctly Mediterranean. Its similar soils to the Alta, particularly the iron traces that give them the ochre red colour, the hotter weather and lower rainfall, yield deep bodied reds with plenty of alcohol but low acidity, which makes them ideal for fleshing out the wines of the other two regions, but means that on their own they do not tend to last long.

A third permutation lies in the grape varieties. The permitted white grape varieties are predominantly the fresh and fragrant Viura, the fragrant Malvasia with its good acidity, and the coarser, higher in alcohol Garnacha Blanca. The red varieties are led by the scented, balanced Tempranillo, the full bodied Garnacha, the perfumed, fresh Graciano, and the Mazuelo, with its colour and tannins.

For red wines, the growers in the Alavesa tend to favour Tempranillo, those in the Alta both Tempranillo and Garnacha, depending on the soils, and the Baja favours the higher yielding Garnacha, which appreciates the hotter weather.

Within each area there are lesser but still recognisable differences in the wines coming from different microclimates, and a skilled blender will be able to spot these differences, giving him or her the possibility of even further permutations in producing the final blend.

When the Rioja was firmly nudged into the twentieth century a little over a decade ago, most of the important bodegas embraced modern winemaking methods for their red wines. A few, those that Hugh Johnson calls the 'conservative bodegas', clung to the old way of making their red wines. Riscal, Lopez de Heredia, CVNE, La Rioja Alta, Bilbainas, Muga and Murrieta still ferment the grapes, adding a small percentage of white Viura grapes to increase the acidity (still a commonplace practice throughout the Rioja) in large oak vats, often open at the top, then mature the new wine in large and small oak casks that have seen lengthy service, and hence impart less to the wine than new wood would. Just before bottling the wine is fined (cleaned of any remaining solid particles) by adding egg whites.

However, the vast majority of the important bodegas now ferment their wines in stainless steel or resin-lined concrete tanks under strict temperature control, avoiding contact with the air, and mature their red wines in new or one-year-old small (225 litre) American or Yugoslavian casks. French oak has been tried, but generally doesn't seem to favour Riojan reds, and is vastly more expensive anyway.

These producers have also tended to move away from maturing the wines in oak towards giving them more time in bottle before release, which they reckon gives a wine of greater finesse.

Neither group is right or wrong. The conservatives make some great red Riojas, but so too do the modernists.

However, the modernists have found themselves with one rather surprising advantage over the traditionalists. When they installed their new winemaking equipment, it was for the express purpose of making red wines. However, it occurred to one modernist, Julio Faustino Martinez, that the same equipment could equally be used to make new style white wines. The Rioja had always had white grapes, most of which were mixed in with the red grapes, but some of which went to making white wines, rich golden wines, honeyed with complex oaky flavours that lived to a venerable age. At Lopez de Heredia, who still make such a wine, I once asked how they make it. 'Just as we do our reds' came the reply.

However, these were, and still are, connoisseur's wines of limited production and availability, and not really what the new wine drinker was looking for. Julio Faustino Martinez applied his new winemaking equipment to the Viura grape and in 1976 released a dry, crisp and fresh young, cold fermented white wine, clean and mouth-watering, and just what the market wanted with the swing away from red wine to white wine worldwide. He was soon followed by Marques de Caceres. The other bodegas watched with some astonishment and scepticism until they realised these wines were selling. Now there are thirty-seven bodegas making such a wine.

The conventional wisdom is that these modern whites are made only from Viura grapes, or Viura with some Malvasia. However, I was recently told that no Malvasia is used because it is a grape easily affected by rot. Nevertheless, something like 11 per cent of all Rioja sales are now white wine. Oddly though, the Rioja region is about the only place you will not find them on sale. If the Riojans want something light to drink as an aperitif or on a hot day, they will invariably drink a local rosé. However, their staple diet remains red wine.

A handful of traditionalists still make the old style, deep and wonderful white wines, wines that have spent considerable time in old casks before they are bottled. Murrieta with its famous Ygay, Lopez de Heredia, Muga, Lopez Agos, CVNE and Martinez Lacuesta offer these crianza (wood-aged) whites, and long may they continue to do so. They are classic Spanish wines in every sense, comparable to the fine white Graves wines of Bordeaux.

However, despite the rise of the new whites, the emphasis remains firmly on reds, and here the hapless consumer walks into a small minefield, as there are various grades of quality. The first distinction is a rather arbitrary one between wines called *tinto* or fuller bodied reds, and those called *clarete*, or lighter bodied. However, the same rules apply to both.

The second and much more important distinction is between wines *sin crianza*, or unaged wines in their first or second year that may have had some months in oak, and *con crianza* or wood-aged wines. Most wine drinkers outside Spain would have only tasted aged wines, but within the country, where three-quarters of all the Rioja wine made is consumed, unaged wines accounted for 52 per cent of total sales in 1985.

Within the con crianza category, there are further indications of quality. A red wine labelled con crianza must have been aged for at least two years, of which at least one year is in oak casks. For crianza white and rosé wines, they must spend at least six months in cask.

The higher quality *reserva* red wine must spend at least one year in wood, and a further two years between wood and bottle, and not leave the bodega until the fourth year after the vintage. The producer can, if he wishes, hold the wine for the entire three years in wood, instead of partly in bottle. But he cannot age the wine only in bottle. White and rosé reservas must spend at least six months in wood and be aged for two years in total.

For the highest grade wine, *gran reserva*, wine from a high quality harvest, the wine must spend two years in wood and another three years in bottle, and not leave the bodega until the sixth year after the harvest. A producer can, if he wishes, hold the wine longer in wood and/or bottle, and a good few do. Paternina, for example, still have wine in old casks that goes back to the last century.

For white and rosé gran reservas, the wine must spend at least six months in cask and be aged for four years in total.

These con crianza wines will usually be vintage dated, though the Rioja also allows a producer to declare his wine 2°, 3° or 4° ano on the label, which indicates the length of time it has spent in wood. Under a complex system, however, a 4° ano wine, for example, may not have spent a full four years in wood as the counting begins with the year of harvest, and rolls on another year each 1 January.

This labelling is now largely confined to the home market, and the authorities have made producers also indicate the date of harvest.

There is also a new category of wine labelled *calidad varias cosechas*, which means the wine is a blend of various vintages (cosechas).

Whichever style of wine it is will be indicated on the back label of every bottle of Rioja wine. The first serious regulations governing the making of Rioja wines were not laid down until 1976, but they were rather loose on the subject of ageing. I have heard that some of the older reserva and gran reserva wines are not quite as old as the labels make them out to be, as there was no effective regulation of a bodega's activities.

However, the central government decided to tighten up all the Spanish wine laws, and on 1 August 1979 clear guidelines were laid down for Rioja wines, specifying the minimum ageing times for each category, to apply from the 1980 vintage, and ensuring these rules were adhered to. For wines still held by the various bodegas prior to that vintage, they have to go before a tasting panel to ensure they measure up to reserva or gran reserva quality before they can be released.

It would be very unwise for any bodega to flout these rules today, and the consumer of vintages from 1980 onwards can be sure that at least the minimum ageing requirements have been met. However, the consumer reading the back label of a bottle of Rioja wine should not see that label as an absolute guarantee of quality. The rules covering wood maturation do not define the age or type of wood. A wine aged in new oak will be quite different to one aged in old oak, and there is a lot of old oak in the Rioja, though there is nothing intrinsically wrong with old oak as long as it is kept clean. The label says only that the wine has been in wood for the minimum time.

The same can be said of the length of bottle maturation, which some bodegas regard as far more important than time spent in wood. In theory, at least, the quality of a wine being used to make, say, a reserva wine is dependent on the policy of each bodega. As one producer explained, it was when a wine was bottled that committed him to what designation he gave it.

This rather complex system is, however, adhered to by the major bodegas, for in the end it is the consumer they have to please. And they are not going to risk the reputation of the Rioja and the financial viability of their own bodega for a slight commercial gain.

Most bodegas produce a complete range of different Rioja wines, though, for example, Faustino Martinez make only reserva and gran reserva reds, and others produce only wines from the Alta or Alavesa areas. It is interesting that the two flagships, reserva and gran reserva, account for so little of the total production, 3.6 per cent and 7.2 per cent respectively in 1985, while con crianza wines amounted to 37.3 per cent. Slowly the tide is turning to the better grades, as internationally this is where the Rioja's reputation rests.

There is one other intriguing aspect of the reserva and gran reserva Riojas: their extraordinary longevity. On a visit to

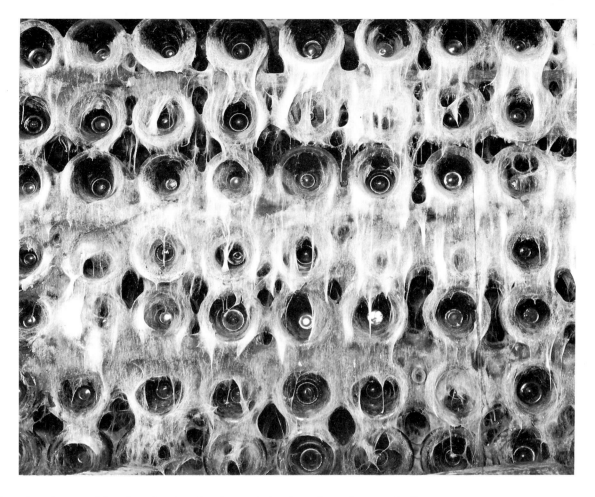

A curious mould enshrouds wines developing in bottle in the underground cellars of Rioja.

Paternina's old cellars in Ollauri the cellar master offered two different wines to his guests and invited us to guess their ages. No one got back beyond the last war. The wines were from the 1870s and 1890s, and still remarkably alive and attractive, when most other wines would have been long dead. I have never been able to get a satisfactory explanation of why Rioja wines are among some of the longest lived in the world.

The skill of the bodegas has much to do with what eventually goes into bottle. Leading bodegas of the Rioja Alavesa include Domecq, Faustino Martinez [who also have revived a local

15

tradition and introduced a 'wine of the year', *vino joven*, made by maceracion carbonique methods to give something akin to a beaujolais nouveau and who have just released their first Cava sparkling wine, Campillo], the brilliant new Martinez Bujanda, the great traditionalists Marques de Riscal, Bodegas Alavesas, Labastida, Palacio, Vina Salceda, Remelluri, Laserna, SMS with their Villabuena label, and El Coto.

The greatest number of bodegas are based in the Rioja Alta. Prominent amongst them are the superb traditionalists Muga, who also produce a Cava wine, Marques de Murrieta, Lopez de Heredia with their Vina Tondonia labels, and the Compania Vinicola del Norte de Espana [CVNE]. The modernists are led by the innovative Marques de Caceres, Montecillo, Olarra, the giant Paternina, Berberana, AGE with their Siglo brand, Lagunilla, Lan, Beronia and Franco Espanolas. Distinguished wines come from La Rioja Alta, Bilbainas, who have a Cava sparkler called Royal Carlton, Corral, Carlos Serres, Gomez Cruzado, Palacios, Martinez Lacuesta, Ramon Bilbao, Bodegas Riojanas, Santa Daria, Campo Viejo, Lopez Agos, Ramon Bilbao, Real Divisa, Velazquez, Cuzcurrita, whose Conde de Alacha has a remarkable Burgundian character, and Santiago.

The handful of bodegas based in the Rioja Baja are Gurpegui, Rivero Ulecia, the giant Savin group and Muerza.

These bodegas have not, unlike some of their neighbours in Penedes, jumped into bed with imported French noble grape varieties. They have decided to stick with their traditional grapes and concentrate on getting the very best from them. A few bodegas have experimental plantings of varieties like Cabernet Sauvignon and Chardonnay, but for the foreseeable future they will not be permitted to plant any more than a few rows of these vines to see how they fare. The likelihood is that grapes from these varieties would be used to give an added dimension to today's wines. Nevertheless, by the turn of the century a handful of innovators may be releasing the first Riojan wines made from French varieties.

For the moment, however, tradition and innovation live happily side by side in the Rioja region. A visitor to the Rioja in 1970 would not have found red wines made in the modern manner, or crisp young white wines for early drinking. But the visitor would have found much that still exists today. The Riojan bodegas have simply grafted the best of the new onto the best of the old.

CHAPTER 3

Navarra

The approach to Pamplona from the west is reminiscent of the drive into Innsbruck in Austria. Craggy steel grey mountains frame high rolling alpine pastures, snow covered in winter, and less suitable land is used for commercial forestry. Here and there are tiny patches of vineyards with stunted, bush–like vines in neat rows. It hardly looks like wine country, yet it is.

Pamplona is the capital of the once formidable Kingdom of Navarra, one of the ancient Spanish kingdoms, now a province in its own right. Like most other historic Spanish cities it has a charming old quarter with unusual architecture that owes more to France than Spain, encircled by the modern highrise apartment blocks preferred by the young.

Each year, during the fiesta of San Fermin between 6 and 12 July, thousands of Basques and visitors from other parts of Spain and abroad descend on Pamplona for the annual running of the bulls. San Fermin was a third–century Christian martyr and patron saint of Pamplona. Each year, by custom, relics of the saint were paraded through the town from the old chapel to the new, together with a procession of bulls. Apparently out of sheer devilment, local youths prodded the bulls to arouse them, while other youths performed passes at them with their scarlet waistbands. By 1717 it had become the annual running of the bulls.

Today the bulls are let loose in the cobbled streets to run to the bullring, while the more daring youths, dressed in white and sporting red sashes, run in front of them. It is very dangerous, but the youths prove their manhood, and the odd one or two lose it at the same time. Then there is recourse to the wines of Navarra.

Apart from a brief period of Moorish domination, from 738 to 750, Navarra remained an independent kingdom, famous for its knights, with its own king until 1512 when it was annexed by the Catholic monarch Ferdinand. But Navarra remained relatively independent until 1841 when it finally became a province of Spain.

The Navarrans have retained that spirit of independence, and when it comes to wine, are going in their own, quite different direction. Which is a little surprising as they are sandwiched between the big guns of Rioja and Penedes.

At the moment, Navarra is best known for its rosé wines. It is the Tavel of Spain, and Tavel rather than Anjou, as the Navarran rosés have the same bone dry character as their cousins across the Pyrenees in the south of France, rather than the sweeter rosés from the Loire valley. However, in another decade Navarra could be known for some quite different wines if developments currently taking place come to fruition.

The denominated area lies almost dead centre in northern Spain, running from the alpine, rather humid foothills of the Pyrenees, down to the semi-arid south that adjoins the Rioja Baja and its Mediterranean climate. To the north it is a series of rolling hills rising to the mountains. In the south it is flattish with mesas carved by erosion, and ochre coloured soils.

It is determinedly agricultural, with pasturing for livestock, forestry, the growing of cereals, fruits, vegetables including asparagus and artichokes, and, of course, the vine.

The famous pilgrim trail (El Camino) to Santiago de Compostella passed through Navarra, and the pilgrims provided a ready market for its wines, as well as spreading its reputation. Legend has it that so much wine was made that the builders of the church in Mendigorria used wine to mix their cement rather than water, which was in short supply.

Today, in volume terms at least, Navarra is one of the smaller producing regions, but it is a healthy and growing industry.

The first moves to denominate Navarra started in 1933, but for a variety of reasons the first rules were not promulgated until 1967, and the denominacion did not come into force till 1975. Currently there are some 20,000 hectares under vine, with another 3,000 hectares technically within Navarra but coming under the Rioja banner.

The region has been divided into five sub-zones. The most northerly, the Baja Montana, covers the Pyrenean foothills of the north-east. It is cool, with plenty of rainfall, and is best suited for light reds, and rosés in particular. Valdizarbe in the central north, to the south of Pamplona, also has a coolish climate but with a slightly lower rainfall than Baja Montana, and produces mainly crianza wines. Tierra Estella to the north west is a little drier, but yields good reds, whites and rosés. All three have predominantly chalky soils, and between them they account for just under 40 per cent of the total production.

The largest area in terms of production is the Ribera Alta, west of Olite, the charming little old-style town with its fairy-tale castle that used to vie with Pamplona as the capital of Navarra. It is drier, somewhat warmer, and gives good red wines, whites and slightly deeper rosés. The driest, warmest zone is the Ribera Baja, to the very south and straddling the Ebro river. Here the reds are full bodied, with plenty of alcohol and colour, and a little sweet white wine is made from the Moscatel grape. Both Riberas have sandy, stony and limestone soils.

The dominant grape of Navarra is Garnacha, the Grenache of the Rhône Valley, and four-fifths of it goes to the making of the rosado or rosé wines. However, the authorities, reacting to consumer tastes, and the need to get better wines that will fetch higher prices, are actively discouraging further plantings of Garnacha in favour of the much better quality Tempranillo, particularly in the cooler northern areas. Two other red grape varieties, Mazuelo and Graciano, are also permitted, and recently Cabernet Sauvignon has been added to the list. The preferred white grape is Viura, but also used are the Malvasia of Rioja, and Moscatel de Grano Menudo for sweet wines.

A Land Reform Act in 1932 created a mass of smallholders, and for many of them grapes were their major cash crop. However few, if any, had any vinification skills or the capital to buy the equipment to make their own wine, so co-operatives sprang up throughout the region, and today continue to dominate the production of Navarran wine. About 92 per cent comes from the co-operatives, the balance from a handful of private but very good producers. Yet these private bodegas, eight or nine in number, have led the way in exporting Navarran wine in bottle, and building a new reputation for Navarra abroad.

What is unusual is the backing all the Navarran grape growers and wine producers are getting from the regional government, and in directions which could change the face of Navarran viticulture and its ultimate reputation for wine.

In 1982, with regional government support and part funding, a private research station was set up in Olite. The Estacion de Viticultura y Enologia de Navarra SA [EVENSA] is virtually unique in Spain, for its brief is to examine every aspect of grape growing and winemaking in the region, as well as to act as the authority certifying the quality of all Navarran export wine. Its laboratories have the best and most expensive analytical equipment available, and throughout the region are substations constantly feeding information about weather patterns, soil types, viral and pest threats and other data into its computer banks.

In 1986, the regional government took full control [becoming known as EVENA], and in 1987 a brand new and very costly experimental winery was opened in an old alcohol factory on the outskirts of Olite. Here the chief oenologist, Javier Ochoa [who also owns his own small bodega], is starting to vinify the grapes from experimental vineyards planted right across Navarra in 1983. Those vineyards were planted not just with native varieties and a handful of imports, but no fewer than 35 different 'foreign' grape varieties, some from other parts of Spain, most from abroad.

The list includes Spanish grapes like the Parellada and Xarel-lo of Penedes, the Airen of La Mancha and the Verdejo of Rueda, French noble varieties including Cabernet Sauvignon, Chardonnay, Pinot Noir, Gamay, Syrah, Chenin Blanc, Pinot Blanc and Gewurztraminer, the Sangiovese and Barbera of Italy, Riesling from Germany, and Thompson Seedless and Ruby Cabernet from California.

The first success has been with Cabernet Sauvignon. It is now authorised, the best bodegas are planting it, and the first red wines with Cabernet in the blend are available. Merlot has been given tentative approval, but has yet to make an impact, and one or two bodegas have experimental plantings of other varieties. Senorio de Sarria has quite a large vineyard of Chardonnay and some Pinot Noir, and elsewhere Gamay and Ugni Blanc are planted.

At the experimental winery, the first wines from this wide spread of varieties have just been vinified, and have not been properly evaluated. Nor will Javier Ochoa be drawn on what varieties he thinks will be successful. However, it is the most wideranging research being done on new varieties in Spain, and the potential is there for a major impact on Navarran viticulture.

Traditions persist in the Rioja region, with old wooden tubs still used to take grapes to the wineries.

Patchwork Rioja vineyards with the modern capital, Logrono, in the background.

The huge estate of Senorio de Sarria, where the government-owned vineyards now include Chardonnay and Pinot Noir.

The artistry of the Catalonians is highly individualistic, as is their approach to winemaking.

New oak barrels have radically reshaped Navarran red wines, and further experiments could bring refinements.

This keynote experiment is just one of many being done by EVENA. Different rootstocks are being tested, different methods of training and pruning the vines, the matching of different varieties to microclimates and soil types, forward warning of fungal and pest infestations in the vineyards, picking times, the best oak for maturing red wines, how long the wine should spend in oak and bottle, what is the ideal blend, how the wine should be fined, whether barrel fermentation should be used, vinification temperatures, whether carbonique maceration is suited to some varieties, and whether the Navarran white grape varieties are suited to making a Cava sparkling wine.

Now the farmer can send his soil for analysis and have his climate monitored, and EVENA will tell him, free of charge, which rootstocks to use, how to improve his soil, which varieties are best suited to his vineyard, and how best the vines should be trained. In some areas the old *poda en vaso* [vase-shaped or Gobelet] bush vines are giving way to *poda en espaldera*, trained vines, those with the cane on wires on the Guyot system.

The winemakers too are getting a mass of information on how to 'fine tune' their wines, on how to make better blends, and generally improve overall quality. In short, EVENA is steering the future of Navarran viniculture, and in a virtually unique way for Spain.

Despite the presence of new and different varieties, it is not the intention of the bodegas to make a Navarran Cabernet Sauvignon or Navarran Chardonnay in the foreseeable future. Rather these new wines will be used to improve the existing blends, as the Cabernet is already doing in the better red wines.

Blending remains the key to Navarran wines. For the reds the four different varieties can be used in differing amounts and from differing sub-zones and wineries. The rosados remain largely Garnacha based, but the styles can vary, and, for example, Sarria even include a small proportion of white Viura juice in their rosado for freshness. The whites vary from pure Viura to half and half with Malvasia, giving a different, softer taste.

Broad generalisations can be made about Navarran wines, but within each category are discernible differences. The white wines are dry, crisp, fresh and very clean. Those from Viura can have a slight waxiness but range from flinty dry, such as those from Sarria, Ochoa, Vinicola Navarra, Romero and Agramont, to the softer, slightly fruitier styles of Irache, Monte Ory, Chivite and Principe de Viana. The lesser wines can also show an earthiness from too much skin contact during fermentation.

The rosados equally range from bone dry to a softer, fruitier style, often with a savoury character at the finish, and certainly with mouthwatering freshness. Those of Irache, Sarria, Ochoa, Romero's Torrecilla and Agramont fall within the former category, while Chivite, Romero's Malon de Echaide and Vinicola Navarra's Las Campanas come within the latter.

The red wines come in two styles: young, fresh, unwooded and gulpable, or crianza [wood matured] wines at three levels: crianza, reserva and gran reserva, which will be indicated on a back label issued by EVENA after analytical and tasting tests.

The crianza reds must, by law, have a minimum two years'

maturation, at least one year in oak casks of no greater than 500 litres capacity. Reserva wines must be three years old, of which at least one year is in cask, while gran reserva wines are at least two years in oak and a further three years in bottle. They are usually made only in the greatest years like 1978, 1981 and 1982.

The unaged reds have a similarity of style. They have a young fruity colour and aroma, fresh and light, and softly fruity on the palate with an easy drinking style, as shown by the Nuevo Vino of Romero, the Irache, Monte Ory, the Bandeo of Vinicola Navarra, the Campo Nuevo of Agramont and its Verjus, or the new Vina Marcos of Chivite.

When it comes to the crianza reds there is more diversity of style based on the different grape proportions used, and the oak. In a blend, the Tempranillo is used for colour and suppleness plus body, and it is interesting that no bodega has bottled it yet as a single varietal, for with proper wood ageing it produces an excellent wine in its own right, and is certainly the best of the four native red varieties.

Garnacha contributes alcohol and body, Graciano gives acidity and fruitiness, and Mazuelo softness and colour. The Cabernet Sauvignon, now being increasingly used, gives an extra dimension in terms of body, aroma and finesse.

As for the oak, most bodegas are using American, though Sarria, for example, uses Limousin from France. Very few bodegas are using new casks, however, though they are regularly cleaned. The barrique is the standard size.

So the overall result depends on what proportions of the different varieties are used. Basically it is a split between Tempranillo and Garnacha, with Mazuelo and Graciano running at around 10 to 20 per cent. The better wineries go more for Tempranillo, and this can be picked up through the drier flavour it imparts, and a distinct savoury tang at the finish of the palate.

Across the board the crianza and reserva wines distinguish themselves through a sweetness on the end palate, almost a portiness that is not unobjectionable but is noticeably there. It comes from the Garnacha. The gran reservas, however, are very different. They tend to be bigger, firmer and drier, with a spicy, peppery character from the oak, and a smooth suppleness. They are wines that will keep for many years, and have some affinity with a decent, mature claret, which may have something to do with the Bordeaux influence on the region which dates back to the last century.

Red wine still constitutes the largest output of Navarra, though it was briefly overtaken by rosé in 1984. However, its production is falling, and whereas three times as much red wine as rosé was made in 1974, now the gap has narrowed and for every eight litres of rosé wine, only eleven of red are made. Rosé will probably win in the end. White wines are minuscule in quantity, about 5 per cent of the total, but the growth is upwards.

The myriad of tiny, patchwork vineyards, and the pervasive influence of the co-operatives of Navarra, somewhat distort its image in that the best-known wines come from the handful of private producers, one or two leading co-operatives and the regional government itself.

The Chivite family, Don Julian, sons Julian, Carlos, Fernando and daughter Mercedes, are the current members of a family that have been making Navarran wine since the eighteenth century. Their Gran Fuedo, Vina Marcos and Parador Chivite [named after the old coaching house where the family still live] labels are the most widely exported, and the family is about to double the capacity of its bodega.

Senorio de Sarria is the brilliant creation of the late construction magnate Felix Huarte who, in 1952, took over 1,500 hectares of abandoned land and turned it into a model estate including his own chateau styled on Bordeaux lines, a complete village for the estate workers with its own priest, doctor, pelota court and school, cinema and swimming pool, and a model winery based on 150 hectares of vineyards. It is more than ten kilometres to the winery from the entrance to the estate, and all in all it has 55 km of private road.

The Huarte family still own the estate, but the vineyards and winery are now owned by the regional Navarran government. They are also involved in wine through CENALSA, a marketing operation that via its own oenologists tells growers when to pick, selected co-operatives how to make the wine, then takes over the bottling, maturation and marketing of the wines through its Agramont, Principe de Viana and Ventana labels. With one or two exceptions, it was CENALSA that started the move towards exporting bottled wine, when two or three years ago most went in bulk to other regions like Catalonia.

Vinicola Navarra, with its Las Campanas and Bandeo labels, Irache [which means Land of Ferns], a bodega framed by a monastery begun in the fifth century and which once housed a famous medical school, the tiny Ochoa where Javier Ochoa and his family live on the top floor, have their offices on the ground floor and the winery in the basement, Bardon and Carricas, together with the major co-operative Nuestra Senora del Romero, are the other important exporters.

It is a tiny group, but one that lives in a part of Spain where some of the most exciting vinous developments are taking place, and where the future has no limits.

CHAPTER 4

Catalonia

Penedes

In the minds of most informed wine drinkers, the Penedes region is where the Spanish viticultural revolution began, and the Penedes remains its heartland. However this is not quite the case. Despite the local Consejo Regulador endorsing the planting of ten 'foreign' grape varieties alongside the native ones, the growers have not rushed to plant them, nor have the majority of bodegas shown any great enthusiasm for making wine from them. These imported varieties still only account for 5 per cent of total plantings, only a drop in the wine vat.

What has happened is that a brilliantly sustained information campaign by the Torres family, who have led and continue to lead the 'modernisation' of the Penedes wine industry, has tended to spread the belief that the other Penedes wineries are doing what Torres is doing. In fact they are not. The Torres family is unique in the context of the Spanish wine industry, and while they have extolled the virtues of the Penedes and its wines, they have, consciously or unconsciously, built the name Torres into a brand name, not necessarily associated with Penedes, or even Spain for that matter, in the eyes of the average wine drinker.

What is important about the Penedes is that what the Torres family, Jean Leon and a handful of other experimentalists have been doing has filtered out to other parts of the Spanish wine industry and been enthusiastically adopted by other adventurous winemakers and vineyard owners in other regions, and hence the excellent crop of new and interesting wines that are starting to come out of Spain.

Viticulturally these changes embrace wider concepts like the importance of cool climate growing to enhance flavours and life giving acidity in wines, coupled with lower alcohol levels, through the importance of microclimates and the matching of different vine varieties to the ideal climate and soil patterns, right down to clonal selection to get the best and sturdiest examples of each variety, the density of planting, the way the vine is trained and pruned, irrigation methods, even the density of the foliage of each vine and the number of bunches of grapes it will be allowed to bear.

In the wineries the Penedes has been at the forefront of the introduction of stainless steel, cold fermentation, the use of better yeast strains, the introduction of new, small oak casks to mature both red and white wines, more emphasis on bottle maturation, and perhaps above all the awareness of how imported varieties can be used, through blending, to give an extra dimension to the wines formerly only made from native grapes.

In short, the science of modern winemaking came to Spain via the Penedes, and hence its importance.

It is, however, a modern revolution in a region with a long history of winemaking. The trading posts on the Catalan coast saw adventurers from Ancient Greece, Carthage and Phoenicia settle and plant vines. But it was the Romans, colonising what they knew as Tarraconensis, who spread the art of viticulture. Despite several barbarian invasions, the sound base for winemaking laid by the Romans was not destroyed until the arrival of the Moors in 711, and though they were not finally driven out of the region till 1099, a modest revival had already begun in the tenth century.

Viticulture flourished and expanded from the twelfth to fourteenth centuries, declined again, only to rise once more at the end of the seventeenth century. When phylloxera hit the vineyards of France, Catalonian wine exports boomed, but the vine louse made its way to the Penedes and from 1876, four years after Josep Raventos introduced the first Cava sparkling wine, now a massive industry, the infection began its deadly work on the vineyards.

Stainless steel and cool fermentation is essential to make delicate white wines. Fortunately steel is cheap in Spain.

Replanting and recovery this century was slow, and more attention focused on the development of the Cava wine industry. Its sparkling wines were drunk throughout Spain, but the Penedes table wines mainly went to the tables of Barcelona and the resorts of the Costa Brava. The international recognition of the Penedes as a high quality table wine producing area really goes back only to the early 1970s.

The denomination of origin Penedes now covers some 25,000 hectares of vines, much of it providing grapes for the Cava wine industry, which is, however, legally permitted to bring in wine from other parts of Spain, while the table wine producers are not.

The region has been further subdivided into the Penedes Superior, the Medio Penedes and the Baja Penedes, based on climatic conditions. The flat coastal lands of the Baja Penedes gradually give way to the undulating Medio Penedes, then rise to the foothills of the Cordillera Litoral Catalana coastal mountain range and the jagged Montes de Garraf to the east, the Penedes Superior zone where vines grow up to an altitude of 800 metres.

The smallest of the three regions, the Penedes Superior has been the focus of recent attention. With a climate comparable to the Rhine Valley, Champagne or the coolest parts of the Napa Valley, it is ideal for growing the Parellada grape to give delicate white wines, and on an experimental basis for varieties like Riesling and Pinot Noir which prefer cooler growing conditions. Interestingly, it has proved too cool for Cabernet Sauvignon.

The Medio Penedes or middle region, a broad belt from Pont del Diable in the east to Stes Creus in the west, and with the table wine capital Vilafranca del Penedes as its epicentre, is where around 60 per cent of the table wine grapes are grown. Its undulating hills up to 200 metres offer a succession of microclimates, but basically the cooler parts equate with Bordeaux or the Sonoma Valley and its warmer zones with the upper Napa or Tuscany.

The flat Baja Penedes, the warmest zone inland from the coast, can be compared climatically with California's Central Valley and Jerez. It is hot enough to allow the growers around the holiday resort of Sitges to carry on an old tradition and allow Malvasia grapes to shrivel on the vine, giving a rich dessert wine called Malvasia of Sitges, though today only in tiny quantities. Generally the area produces full bodied wines for adding depth to standard blends.

Only certain grape varieties can be grown throughout the Penedes. The white varieties are led by Parellada, the best of these varieties, which yields a crisp, aromatic, delicate white wine. Macabeo, a vine that gives good yields, produces a fruity wine with good acidity. Xarel-lo gives a somewhat neutral wine but with good body, which is why it is the mainstay of the Cava industry. Subirat-Parent, White Garnacha, Malvasia, Pansé and Pedro Ximinez are also permitted but have faded in importance.

The native red grape varieties grown are led by Ull de Llebre or Tempranillo, giving a wine of good colour, alcohol and acidity, ideal for laying down. Garnacha Tinta gives smooth, fruity young wines, and its cousin Garnacha Peluda is also grown in small quantities. Monastrell gives wine with a deep colour and elegant flavour, while Carinena gives full-bodied wines of good colour, which make them ideal for blending. Sumol gives a light, aromatic wine for use in young, fresh blends for immediate drinking.

When it comes to both red and white imported varieties, the Penedes Consejo operates a three-tier system. Only Chardonnay and Cabernet Sauvignon have full status and can be bottled as such and carry the denomination of origin Penedes.

A second group hold a temporary visa in that they can be planted and used in blends, but not bottled as such with the denomination of origin. They are Riesling, Sauvignon Blanc, Gewurztraminer, Muscat d'Alsace and Muscat d'Hambourg, Pinot Noir and Merlot.

The third group can only be planted on an experimental basis and include Chenin Blanc, Petite Syrah and Cabernet Franc.

There are no hard and fast rules about how each winery can use this panoply of varieties, both local and imported, but the vast majority of table wines coming out of Penedes are blends of two or more varieties. The exception is the growing number of fresh young white wines now being made only from Parellada. Torres do two, the dry Vina Sol and the off dry San Valentin, but out of their product range of thirteen wines, only four are single varietal wines, the two mentioned, the branded Waltrud which is made from Riesling grapes, and their flagship red Gran Coronas Black Label, which is pure Cabernet Sauvignon.

So the visitor to Penedes will be hard pressed to taste the different local varieties outside tank samples at the wineries. However one small bodega did make a habit of bottling the four main white varieties as single wines, while also using them to make a blend. At the bodega of Herredad Montsarra, a tasting of these four wines made by the Jané family showed Parellada has nothing to fear as the king of white grapes in this part of the world. With a delicately flowery and aromatic aroma, and a crisp, flinty flavour, it finished fruity and clean.

Macabeo showed a leafier, more herbaceous aroma, and a fuller but quite grassy flavour with a slightly hard edge to it. Xarel-lo showed a crisp, clean wine but lacking in personality, while Subirat-Parent had a quite sappy aroma and greenish flavour.

The reason why so relatively few single varietal wines are made in the Penedes seems to be two-fold. First, blending is how the industry traditionally made its wines, and most bodegas see no reason to change, believing the sum of the parts are preferable to the parts alone.

The second reason lies in the infrastructure of the local industry. The majority of vineyards are family owned. Throughout the region are patches of stubbly vineyards, the gnarled trunks and branches of each vine protruding barely a metre above ground. That is why it is so easy to spot the vineyards of the more progressive wineries, with their wired trellises and higher trained vines.

Some growers are under contract to different bodegas and are helped and encouraged by them. But most belong to the local co-operative. The co-operative movement started in the Penedes in 1906 with the formation of El Vendrell. Others followed and the list now includes the likes of Covides, Espluga, La Granada, Pla de Santa Maria, La Bisbal, Les Cabanyes, Sant Jaume del Domenys, l'Arboc, Vilafranca, Llorens, Banyeres and Aiguamurcia. These are large operations, and most are now thoroughly modernised and under the direction of skilled winemakers.

They buy in and vinify their members' grapes, both for the Cava producers and the table wine bodegas. With the exception of Vilafranca with its very good Reserva Especial and Reserva Especial Macabeo, or l'Arboc with its equally good Castell de Caldera, these co-operatives are not in the business of bottling wine. They make it and sell it, usually in the blended form. Only the tiniest bodegas are self-sufficient in grapes, so most buy in wine from the co-operatives for maturation, bottling and marketing under their own name. It would be difficult for them to develop large stocks of single varietal wines even if they wanted to.

What has been exciting in the last decade and a half has been not only the introduction of new wines, but more importantly the marked improvement of existing wines. The introduction of cold fermentation has brought a host of fresh, crisp and fruity white wines, well suited to the modern drinker, and in an area where white wine production accounts for something like 80 per cent of the total it was a much needed innovation. Increasing use of new and better wood has given added complexity to the red wines, and a better understanding of the whole science of winemaking, coupled with the fine tuning that can now be done in modern laboratories, has put the stamp of quality on the Penedes reds.

The importation and planting of foreign varieties has had far

31

less impact. Torres are using Chardonnay, Sauvignon Blanc, Gewurztraminer, the two Muscats, Riesling, Cabernet and Pinot Noir in their wines. Jean Leon and Mont Marcal use Chardonnay and Cabernet Sauvignon, Cavas Hill have planted Chardonnay, Parato Vinicola use some Pinot Noir, Manuel Sancho has tiny amounts of a straight Cabernet, and Jose Alegret, Jose Freixedas, Masia Bach, Masia Vallformosa, Conde de Caralt and Rene Barbier all use some Cabernet Sauvignon in their top red wines.

Still a drop in the ocean, this movement is gathering a little force. It began in 1967 when the Catalonian-born Jean Leon, owner of the La Scala restaurant in Beverly Hills, returned to his native land and began planting Cabernet Sauvignon in some old vineyards he had bought. He subsequently added Chardonnay, Cabernet Franc and Merlot to his vineyards.

Jean Leon's intention was to make wine he could sell to his California customers from his homeland. But Californians have a Californian taste in wine, so to be successful he needed to develop along those lines, hence the use of noble varieties to make his red and white wine. At around the same time Miguel Torres Jnr graduated from the famous oenological university at Montpellier in France and persuaded his successful father Don Miguel to let him plant experimental vineyards of imported vines. The resulting new white wines, and then the reds, convinced the family this was the path to follow.

If the Torres family, father Miguel, sons Miguel Jnr and Jaime, and daughter Marimar, tend to hog the headlines, they thoroughly deserve to do so. Their path was fraught with danger, and it took much hard work to win over a wider audience to their wines, and in doing so alerting that audience to the fact that something was going on down in Penedes. Winemaker Miguel Jnr is an innovator in both the vineyards and the winery. He is respected by winemakers in many other parts of the world.

In the family vineyards, and those that supply the winery, he has instituted a range of reforms: matching varieties to microclimates, improved rootstocks, clonal selection, new training methods, correct harvesting times, particularly for white grape varieties, and so on. It takes time for these developments to filter out. A private grower takes a lot of convincing to make the capital investment involved in replanting and then waiting three years to get his next harvest so the winemaker will get better grapes to make better wine.

The Californian winery owner would feel quite at home at the modern Torres winery. The best presses, self drainers, banks of stainless steel fermenters, centrifuges, and an underground chai stuffed with top quality oak barrels, show the determination of the family to get the best out of their grapes.

Miguel Torres constantly searches for that little extra. His latest experiment is with a stainless steel drum with, at each end, the conventional oak end of a Bordeaux barrel. He is trying to see if it will give the oak flavours he wants in his red wines, perhaps over a slightly longer period, but ultimately at a fraction of the cost. The horrendous cost of new oak casks, which in a modern winery are usually replaced every two years, means that after the initial cost of the stainless steel, he would only have to replace the oak ends after each cycle at far less cost. If it works, this development could spread far and wide.

Modern filling equipment is now essential for the big exporters of Spanish wines.

The flagship Torres wines, Gran Vina Sol, Gran Vina Sol Green Label, Vina Magdala, Gran Coronas and Gran Coronas Black Label, and their popular wines like Vina Sol, Vina Esmeralda and Tres Torres, and their fine Catalan brandy, have bought the family their share of success. They are constantly expanding their vineyard holdings in Penedes, have now established a second vineyard in Chile, and are starting a third in California. Their search for quality goes on.

Jean Leon's enterprise has flourished too, though on a far smaller scale. His small but modern winery still produces just Chardonnay and Cabernet Sauvignon, though the latter now has some Cabernet Franc in the blend. The Chardonnay is barrel fermented then matured in oak to give a distinctly un-Penedes, Californian buttery rich aroma and full, oaky flavour. It is also given quite a long time in bottle before release, as is his Cabernet Sauvignon, which sees the two Cabernets vinified separately in temperature controlled cement vats, blended, then going into new or one-year oak for at least two years. The result is again Californian with a deep colour, firm dry oaky varietal aroma and deep, concentrated flavour. Its only rival in the Penedes is the more Bordeaux-styled Torres Gran Coronas Black Label.

The other leading bodegas have basically concentrated on native grape varieties, particularly Parellada, to make new-wave white wines. On the whole they tend to be very fresh, clean and light, with a delicate aroma, and crisp, mouthwatering acidity, sometimes lemony or grassy, and all best drunk when young. Some also have a little toughness or earthiness.

Typical good examples are Kraliner from Rene Barbier, the table wine arm of Cava producers Segura Viudas, two other still wines from Cava houses in Vin Nature Blanc de Blancs of Marques de Monistrol and Blanc Brut from Cavas Hill, Bosch Guell Blanco, the Primer Vi Novell of Mont Marcal, Vina Laranda Blanco from Ferret & Mateu, the Junot of Jaime Lluch Casanellas, the Vino Blanco Seco of Jose Alegret and Montgros Blanc from Aquila Rossa.

To my mind these wines have a distinct edge over the rival new-wave Rioja white wines which may be partly due to climate, but more likely to the suitability of the Parellada to make white wines against the Rioja's Viura. However the Rioja has the consolation of being well ahead in the general quality of its red wines. Nevertheless there is room for both.

Other white wines of note include the excellent single vineyard wine Blanc Flor Emita d'Espiells of Cava producers Juvé y Camps, a much fuller style of white wine, held in bottle for two years before release, and capable of even further development. Another Cava producer, Manuel Sancho, makes an almost Burgundian Blanco Reserva from his own vineyards that is given several years' bottle maturation before release, and is most unusual in its style. Mont Marcal have Blanco Anada, a vintage dated wine that is usually a little older and drier than most when it goes on release. And of course there is the Extrisimo Gran Reserva dulce of Masia Bach, the lovely old almost Tuscan-style winery now owned by Codorniu. This is one of Spain's best-known dessert wines, though it does not have the richness of a Sauternes, and is complemented by an equally good Extrisimo Seco.

The red wines of Penedes range in style from lightish to medium bodied, fresh younger wines ready for early drinking, and often based on Carinena and Garnacha, of which Sangre de Toro is a perfect, popular example, to deeper, more characterful wines, fuller, robust but usually quite smooth and velvety, based on the noble Tempranillo, and quite capable of bottle improvement. Some examples are Masia Bach Tinto, the Vall Reserva of Masia Vallformosa, the Tinto Alegret of José Alegret, the Gran Toc Reserva of Cavas Hill, the Tinto Abocado of Marques de Monistrol, the Cabernet Sauvignon of Mont Marcal, the Chateldon Reserva of Bodegas Pinord, the nicely oaked Rene Barbier Reserva, Conde de Caralt Reserva, or the vintage dated Freixedas Tinto.

What does the rest of the twentieth century hold for Penedes? The answer seems to be a very slow evolution of more new wines, and a gradual acceptance of imported noble varieties. As Miguel Torres Jr has said, it is not hard to sell a competent winemaker stainless steel, show him how to use it, and get pretty rapid, impressive results. It is slower and much harder to change viticultural practices, and the results take time to come through.

Ever so gradually, those private growers who have any foresight are seeing that they will get more money for better quality grapes, and the imported noble varieties are starting to command a premium, so there is a small but important change in the vineyards.

What is uncertain is what changes in wine drinking patterns Spain's accession to the European Economic Community will bring. It has given Spain greater access to the northern markets, but it has also opened up Spain to competition from French and Italian producers. The average closeted Spanish wine drinker has had very little experience of French or Italian wines, and even now

Computerisation means fewer men are now needed to work the modern wineries.

it is rare indeed to see good French wines on sale elsewhere than on the wine lists of the most expensive restaurants.

If, as expected, a younger generation with more disposable income starts to take to a range of hitherto unknown wine flavours like Cabernet Sauvignon, Chardonnay or Sauvignon Blanc, only the Penedes and neighbouring Navarra are far enough down the viticultural road to be in a position to supply such wines from Spain's own vineyards.

The Penedes just might become the Bordeaux and Burgundy of Spain rolled into one. And if you include the Cava sparkling wine industry, it could become France's vineyard in Spain.

Cobwebbed cellars hold reserves of rare old Navarran wines.

Despite the invention of automatic remuage, the old way, turning bottles by hand, is still widely used in the Penedes.

Girosols, or sunflowers, were invented by the Cava industry of Penedes, and are now also used in Champagne.

Cava Wines

The unprepossessing small farming town of San Sadurni de Noya, its small centre surrounded by the dull, squat apartment blocks found throughout the modern Mediterranean, literally sits on a fortune. Beneath its rutted streets are the seemingly endless caverns where millions upon millions of dark green bottles in orderly stacks are bringing to maturity Spain's best-known sparkling wines under the general name Cava.

The casual visitor to San Sadurni, or Sant Sadurni d'Anoia as the roadsign says in Catalan, could hardly guess that this rather unattractive little town is the centre of one of the world's most formidable sparkling wine industries, based on the methode champenoise.

To put the Cava industry into perspective, its annual production is now around 120 million bottles, which is not all that far off Champagne's annual production of around 195 million bottles. Codorniu alone, the largest Cava house, produces 36 million bottles every year, almost a sixth of the total Champagne production, and Freixenet, which has just incorporated the old Rumasa houses into its empire, now exceeds that comfortably as a group.

However Champagne is a delimited region, and its vineyards can only produce a finite amount of wine. Cava wines too can only come from certain areas, but the patch is much larger than that of Champagne, so as demand increases for Cava wines the producers can expand to meet it, an option not readily available to the Champenois.

The Cava industry, despite its size, is only a few years over a century old, whereas Champagne can trace its antecedents back to the late 1600s. The Penedes region of Catalonia has been producing table wine since the Greeks and Phoenicians first planted vines there, but it was not until 1872 that the first methode champenoise sparkling wine was produced by Don Jose Raventos, whose family had been in the wine business since 1551.

Raventos travelled on behalf of the family firm, and while in the Champagne region he closely studied the way its wines were made, and brought the method, and some equipment, back across the Pyrenees to his native Catalonia.

However, Raventos did not bring back the Champagne grape varieties, Chardonnay, Pinot Noir and Pinot Meunier, but applied the techniques he had learnt to the native grape varieties of Penedes. So while the very best sparkling wines being made today in California, the Cape and Australia ape champagne, the Cava wines don't. They have their own special character precisely because they are still made from those native varieties.

The first releases from the Raventos family were extremely successful in Spain, and encouraged others to try their hand. Now there are scores of companies making Cava wines, although more than half of the total production comes from the cellars of Codorniu and Freixenet.

The grapes for Cava wines largely come from the Penedes region, though under new regulations, still wine or must can be purchased outside Penedes from other, approved regions of Spain.

Some of the smaller houses rely entirely on their own vineyards for the grapes they need, but the bigger ones buy in large quantities of grapes from the many small farmers who work the Penedes land, farmers whose tiny plots are handed down from generation to generation, and whose patches of vineyard run alongside small crops of wheat and other cereals, and a bit of land for the odd pig, cow or sheep. They may look like peasants, but their children probably have a small apartment in town, go to better schools than their parents ever dreamed of, and who will enjoy a better standard of living thanks to the demand for Cava wines.

The vineyards in winter look like rows of grey hands clawing out of the earth, stubby and usually less than a metre high. Trellising the vines on wires is a rare sight throughout the Penedes, and has only been introduced by the more experimental table winemakers over the last decade. In summer the stubbly vines with their leaf cover are protected by their size from the ravages of the Levant, which can hit this part of the Spanish coast, and the warm soil at night helps ripen the grapes. However frost is another danger in this region, and in some years it can slash production from vines so close to the ground.

The permitted varieties for Cava wines are Parellada, Macabeo, Malvasia, Chardonnay and Xarel-lo, and the red grape Sumoll, which when vinified off the skins can add a little freshness to the wine, and Monastrell, Carinena and Garnacha in small quantities to make pink Cavas.

The majority of these vines are planted in the chalk and clay soils of the middle Penedes. Picking usually starts in early October,

A huge old wine press reminds visitors to a Cava house of the great changes that have come to the industry.

backbreaking work because of the size of the vines, and the new grapes are taken to the wineries in special plastic containers to avoid loss of juice. The growers fix a minimum price in advance for their grapes with the buyers for each winery. Many have what is known locally as a 'moral contract' with a particular Cava house that has passed down through the generations, and ensures that they will only sell their grapes to that house. The arrival on the scene of the giant Rumasa group in the early 1970s and the rapid expansion of their Cava houses sent a shiver through San Sadurni as Rumasa tried to get the grapes it needed by offering higher prices, so inducing growers to break the moral contract. However most growers remained loyal, and the departure of Rumasa has bought stability back to this rather quaint custom. Visitors to Codorniu can see the large old tree outside the main gates where every year the growers and the buyers meet to strike their annual bargain.

The rising demand for Cava wines, and the increasing prosperity it has engendered, has allowed the wineries, both large and small, to invest in new equipment, and the Cava industry is now as modern as any in its winemaking techniques.

After crushing, the grapes go into modern Willmes or Vaselin presses. Only the first pressing juice can be used for Cava wines by law, the remaining juice being disposed of elsewhere. Only a maximum of 150 kilograms of grapes can be used to obtain a hectolitre of must.

The must is then put into holding tanks for twenty-four hours to throw off its solids, and then fermentation takes place. In the past this would have been done in oak *barricas*. Now it is done in stainless steel tanks of varying size or resin-lined concrete vats, both with strictly controlled temperature levels, usually somewhere between 15 and 18 degrees Centigrade. Fermentation usually lasts around ten days: what the winemaker is hoping to achieve is a new still wine of between 10.5 and 12 degrees alcohol, and acid levels of 6 grammes per litre or more to give the best Cava wine. Once fermentation is complete the new wine is chilled to below zero Centigrade to precipitate its tartrates.

The next stage in the process is, as in Champagne, the all important one, the blending of the base wines. The practice is to vinify each grape variety separately, then blend them according to the style each producer wishes to achieve. Parellada contributes finesse and softness, Macabeo gives delicacy and fruitiness to the bouquet, and Xarel-lo the backbone and colour onto which the other two are grafted.

The percentages vary from one wine to another in each house, and from one house to another. So for example Codorniu's Non Plus Ultra is 50 per cent Macabeo, 40 per cent Parellada and 10 per cent Xarel-lo, while Freixenet's Cordon Negro is 29 per cent Macabeo, 38 per cent Parellada and 33 per cent Xarel-lo.

Once the blend is made up it goes into stout bottles, able to withstand the build-up of pressure, and a little *licor de tiraje,* a mixture of cane sugar and wine from the last vintage, is added. The bottle is then sealed with a modern crown cap, rather than corks held in by grapas or wire hooks, which have now largely gone out of fashion because of the cost.

The bottles are taken down into the cavernous cellars below ground where they are stacked in the French method, *sur latte*, with thin slats to keep the necks horizontal, a highly skilled job as the stacks often rise above head height, and are an impressive sight.

The injection of the *licor de tiraje* triggers off the second fermentation, converting the sugars into the carbon dioxide that gives the wine its sparkle. The fermentation period is determined, to some extent, by the temperature of the cellar. The Consejo Regulador de Los Vinos Espumosos, which governs the production of all Spanish sparkling wines, lays down a minimum period of nine months before the next stage, degorgement, takes place, but for most houses this stage can last three or four years, as the longer the wine stays in the bottle, the smaller, finer and more persistent the beads will be, the yeastier the aroma and flavour, the fuller, more complex the taste, the better knit its component parts. That all adds up to superior quality.

Before the process of degorgement comes the process of remuage. The second fermentation throws off dead yeast cells which must be removed from the wine: as they are too fine to be removed by filtration, another way has been developed in Champagne, and is now an integral part of the method.

The bottles are taken from their stacks and placed in racks called pupitres made of wood, or in some instances in Cava country, from stone quarried from the cellars. The pupitres have holes into which the bottles are slotted in a just off horizontal angle. Day by day, over several months, each bottle is given a gentle shake, a quarter turn, and is gradually elevated to a near vertical position, by skilled workers called remuers who can handle 20,000 to 30,000 bottles a day. They are not men to arm wrestle with!

Gradually the yeasts slide down to rest on the crown cap, forming a sandy yellow sludge. To get it out, the degorgement process comes into play. In the past it was hand done. Now it is automatic. The bottles are taken, vertically, and placed neck down into holes on a moving, usually metal belt, and are passed through a bath of liquid nitrogen with about the first half inch of the bottle neck immersed. At minus 20 degrees Centigrade, it freezes the sediment solid.

The cap is flicked off. Whoosh, out shoots the plug of dead yeasts and a little wine, thanks to the pressure in the bottle. It is quickly topped up with a little *licor de expedicion*, in goes a proper champagne cork, and the wire clip that holds it in place is applied.

The process of remuage is one of the reasons why a bottle of methode champenoise wine, from wherever it comes, is always going to be more expensive than a sparkling wine made by one of the other available methods. It is, by its very nature, labour intensive, and therefore costly. The cost-conscious Spanish, competing with their Cava wines as much on price as quality, have developed an alternative system that has now been adopted even by some Champagne houses. It is a semi-automatic or automatic form of remuage, based on a metal device called a *girosol* (sunflower in Spanish) that was developed by Freixenet, and first used by them in the 1970s. It is a square metal frame holding 504 bottles on an octagonal base, set on rockers rather like those of a rocking chair. Two men, each day, give the cradle one eighth of a turn and the angle of the rockers is gradually adjusted. The end result is that the bottles finish up in the same position as they would by hand remuage.

This ingenious Catalan invention has, in some houses, notably Freixenet, been further improved by wiring them to a computer system and a mechanical device that I have not fully come to terms with. The computer issues the instructions, and the machine turns the girosol. They all make an eighth turn, like sunflowers following the sun, which I suppose is how they got their name.

Freixenet say that their research shows absolutely no variation in quality from wine remuaged by hand and that in the girosols. But in practice the best quality wines are still turned in the pupitres, even though the girosols are increasingly widely used throughout the industry.

The *licor de tiraje,* added just before the final corking, and in a very small amount, is a mixture of sugar, old white wine and brandy. The exact amount of sugar determines the final style of wine, for as in Champagne, San Sadurni produces a variety of Cava wines in gradations of dryness.

From driest to sweetest, and for the technically minded the permitted grammes per litre of sugar, they are Brut Natur or Extra Brut [0–6], Brut or Dry [less than 15 grammes], Seco or Extra Dry [12–20], Semi Seco or Dry, but in reality lightly sweet [17–35], Semidulce or Semi Sweet [33–55] and Dulce or Sweet [over 50 grammes].

Once the wine is bottled it is, theoretically, ready for release, and at the least expensive levels of quality, a good bit of it goes out onto the market. But for the superior cuvees the wine goes back to its cellars where extra bottle maturation will improve its quality.

Within this context, each house will also have its different wines, ranging from its bread and butter wines to its prestige cuvees and vintage dated sparklers. To a more sophisticated palate, already accustomed to champagne, it is the two driest styles that will most please; however, among the rosado [pink] Cavas and the slightly sweeter styles, there are some very well made wines that are ideal for certain occasions and certain foods.

Prior to the formation of the Consejo Regulador to govern sparkling wines in July 1972, there was a great deal of sparkling wine floating about that described itself as *champagna,* but had nothing in common with true champagne or the quality Cava wines. Everything was lumped together under the general heading *vinos espumosos.* With the introduction of the regulatory body, clear guidelines were laid down as to what was what. The name Cava was adopted from the same term used to describe the cellars of the methode champenoise producers, as the general name for these wines. They were distinguished by a star with four points on the cork.

Then there are the other sparkling wines, in descending order of quality. First, there are those made by what is known as the transfer method, where first fermentation takes place in bottle, second fermentation in tank. They are distinguished by a rectangle on the cork. Granvas wines, made by the cuve close or Charmat process, where the whole process takes place in tanks, have a circle on the cork, and the very cheap and usually repugnant *vino gasificado,* where carbon dioxide is injected into the wine to make it fizzy, the old bicycle pump method, has a triangle on the cork.

In each instance the way the wine is made must appear on the label: Cava, fermented in bottle, Granvas, *vino gasificado*; a producer of one is not allowed to make any of the others in the same cellar.

In a way it was fortuitous that these changes took place, particularly the creation of Cava as a generic name, and the heavy promotional budget invested in it to encourage consumer awareness of just what Cava is and means. With a neat flanking move during the negotiations over Spain's entry into the European Economic Community, the French managed to get for the Champenois the sole rights to the term methode champenoise, and over the next several years all other producers using the method will have to come up with a different way of describing their wines, if they wish to sell them in the EEC and other countries that have agreed to let the Champenois have sole rights to the name champagne.

It will not matter one whit in countries like the United States and Australia, which have never agreed to the demands of the Champenois, but it caught producers in countries like Italy on the hop, and there is a lot of head scratching going on there. With a strong, already established identity, however, the Cava producers are ideally poised to take advantage of the change of rules. And with demand for champagne already outstripping supply, the strength and size of the Cava industry points to a healthy future.

If there is one factor that could mitigate against Cava wines it is their very distinctive taste, and I am in two minds as to whether it is a plus or a minus factor. Even if they are both made by the same method, there is no mistaking a Cava wine for champagne. In countries like the United States, Australia, the Cape and, closer to home, Italy, the top quality sparkling wines are made from the same grapes as champagne: Chardonnay, Pinot Noir and Pinot Meunier, in emulation and in deference to the great wine. The Cava grapes, however, particularly the Parellada, give a quite different aroma and flavour, with the hallmark being a distinct earthiness to the aroma and flavour, what the French call *gout de terroir*. For some it is a difficult taste to get used to, others like it, but to a greater or lesser degree the Cava wines have it.

Though the industry is a relatively young one, there are now 46 Cava houses of varying size, some like Cavas Hill and Juve I Camps who also make table wine. Unlike many other regions of Spain, most of these companies are in private hands, and the local co-operatives rarely bottle under their own name and play a subsidiary role to these private houses. As yet, the industry has not really spread its wings outside Catalonia, and the only other producers of any note that are not Penedes are Perelada, who have a range of five wines including Gran Claustro from their base in Ampurdan to the north, and three Riojan houses in Bilbainas with Royal Carlton, Muga with Conde de Haro, and Faustino Martinez who have just launched their own Campillo Cava wine.

Within Spain a distinction is made between what are known as the industrial Cava houses, and the artisanal bodegas. The former houses, the very large ones like Codorniu, Freixenet and Segura Viudas, can, because of their very size, achieve a consistency of style in their wines from one year to the next.

The artisanal bodegas like Mestres or Masachs produce wines that show much more variation in character, reflecting the variations in grape quality from vintage to vintage. So in the year of a good harvest they will make better wines than they do in a poor year.

The first Cava house the visitor sees as he enters San Sadurni from the slip road off the main highway is Freixenet, founded in 1887, only a few years after Codorniu, and now one of the two major houses, in fact the largest if one takes in Segura Viudas, Castellblanch and Conde de Caralt, the three former Rumasa bodegas that Freixenet bought from the Spanish government in the summer of 1984. Those three Cava houses are, however, retaining their separate identities and are made at a different winery outside town.

The Freixenet winery, a massively impressive operation that never seems to stop growing, produces a full range of Cava wines of which their Brut Nature, their Cordon Negro Brut in its distinctive black frosted bottle, and the recently introduced premium cuvee Brut Barrocco, vintage dated and less Cava than most in its style, are the best known.

Codorniu is based on the other side of San Sadurni in an extraordinary *fin de siècle* building designed by the Catalan architect Jose Cadafalch, which, in Britain at least, would probably be described as a folly, but which harmonises with the surrounding gardens, ponds and walkways.

Beneath those gardens are their massive cellars, built on five levels, stretching for a staggering 16 miles, and in which, at any one time, they will have something in the region of 125 million bottles undergoing the various stages of the Cava process. Visitors are shown a fraction of these cellars by a mini train whose rear carriages swing dangerously close to the stacks of bottles as the drivers hurl them round corners with a skilled but abandoned air.

At the moment Codorniu has a slight edge over Freixenet in that they can draw on the vast vineyards of the family that are planted with noble French varieties in the seemingly inhospitable plains of the neighbouring province of Lerida. The result is the very recent introduction of two new wines, Anna de Codorniu Brut Reserva and Raimat [the name of the Lerida estate] Blanc de Blancs Brut Nature, both with Chardonnay in the cepage.

Anna de Codorniu, named after an earlier member of the family, has 15 per cent Chardonnay, but the Raimat Blanc de Blancs has a massive 85 per cent, with the balance Macabeo and Parellada. In both instances the result is a much steelier, mouthwatering style of wine, with the earthiness very much pushed into the background, and a fresh cleanliness more to the fore.

Other producers too have access to Chardonnay, but in the foreseeable future few, if any, will be taking a leaf out of Codorniu's book, though it will be interesting to see how markets

45

more in tune with the champagne taste react to the two Codorniu babies.

Their third new wine, Premiere Cuvee Brut, is a sort of super Cava from their very best wines, very dry in style, and it backs up their deservedly popular Non Plus Ultra, their Blanc de Blancs, and the vintage dated Brut Classico, as Codorniu's flagship wines.

Third in size is the Segura Viudas group, who operate from a new, very modern bodega in the countryside outside San Sadurni. During the Rumasa years, substantial sums were spent modernising the winery, building superb new maturation facilities, and establishing the brand names.

Segura Viudas was, and is, the flagship house, and their range of quality Cava wines is led by Brut Reserva and Brut Vintage. Conde de Caralt has a range of typical styles including Brut Zero, Brut Nature and Reserva Brut. Castellblanch, forming the triumvirate, lead with the vintage dated Gran Castell, but have been showing success with their Cristal Brut and off dry Cristal Extra. Much smaller in size is Canals y Nubiola, formerly a producer of sparkling wines by the Charmat method, but which was switched to Cava wines by Rumasa and put under the same roof as Segura Viudas. Their best wine is Gran Nubiola. The bodega was also the source of Jean Perico, the label owned by the sherry company Gonzalez Byass, and which is notable for its Frenchness when put alongside other Cava wines.

A most interesting bodega of medium size is Marques de Monistrol. It is based on 320 hectares of vineyards on land owned by the Marques de Monistrol, outside San Sadurni, the largest single wine estate in Catalonia, which provides all the grapes needed for Monistrol's range of ten Cava wines and additional table wines. Of equal interest is that the production of these wines is based on a village on the estate, complete with its own tiny church, where the families who farm the property are born, live and die in a virtually self-sufficient community.

Monistrol, founded in 1882, is one of the oldest Cava houses, but the recent purchase of the business by Martini and Rossi—of vermouth fame—has energised it, and the Monistrol Brut, vintage dated Brut Nature, and off dry Gran Crement Semi Seco are finding a wider audience.

Small can be beautiful too, and while admitting to not having tasted every Cava wine available, there have been some very enjoyable, high quality wines from these smaller houses tasted in the course of duty. Juve I Camps have as their flagship wine in their range of three Cavas the Reserva de la Familia Brut Natural, vintage dated: a very fine wine with a lot more yeastiness, particularly on the nose, than you would find in many competitors.

Masachs, a family business based in nearby Vilafranca, make a very fine Brut Gran Reserva, and their Rosado Cava is one of the best around. They have a second label in Louis Vernier which is finding considerable favour in Barcelona. Cavas Hill, whose cellars still contain the original stone pupitres used when the company was born, have a vintage dated Brut, Sant Manel Brut and Brut de Brut Gran Reserva de Artesania, all bone dry and squeaky clean wines.

Others in the Cava community whose wines can be found outside the immediate vicinity are Carbonell, Mestres, Nadal, Delapierre [a subsidiary of Codorniu] and Masia Vallformosa.

Cava's looming presence in the world of sparkling wines is one of the better Spanish success stories, and with the emphasis very much on quality it has made an important contribution to Spain's growing wine image. Where the Cava boys go next is anyone's guess, but perhaps Freixenet showed the way when they recently bought Henri Abel, a Champagne house.

Alella

The pocket size denominacion Alella, the smallest in Spain and one of Europe's tiniest delimited areas, lies a little over an hour's drive north of Barcelona. It centres on the seaside village of Alella, a summer holiday retreat for Barcelonans escaping the city's heat, and on the hills that rise behind the village.

The homes of the Barcelonans jostle with small patches of land where the local farmers grow carnations for the flower markets, vegetables and vines, while further inland, where there is less pressure from the builders, the vineyards are rather more substantial.

The local Consejo Regulador has decreed that only certain varieties may be grown. Pansa Blanca dominates the white grape varieties, with Xarel-lo, Pansa Rosada and Garnacha Blanca also permitted, and for red wines Garnacha Negra and Tempranillo.

So far there are around 400 hectares under vine, and most of the grapes picked go to the local co-operative Alella Vinicola, on the road into the village. If anything, the presssure from property developers is likely to diminish the area under vine, though the area's reputation for white wines is rising, thanks to the combination of a cool growing period and modern cold fermentation techniques.

To see the Alella Vinicola one would hardly think so. Founded in 1906, and now with around 150 farmer members, the offices are just as they were the day they were built. No chrome and computers here. The winery too, behind the offices, is also a step back in time. Some of the large oak vats, one dating back to the last century, are almost falling to bits with age. Slightly newer concrete fermenters have been insulated for cold fermentation, but stainless steel is not a feature of this winery.

The Alella Vinicola has made something of a speciality of semi-sweet and sweet white wines under its Marfil brand name—soft, slightly peachy wines that are popular locally. However, under the incomprehensible rules of the local denominacion, both red and white wines must spend at least one year in oak. In the case of the co-operative, the wood is generally too old to have much impact on flavour. However, the dry white Marfil Legitimo Blanco Seco does have a hardish flavour and has lost its bounce due to this ageing requirement. The co-operative also produces a respectable rosé and two vintage dated reds of lighter body.

In complete contrast is Alta Alella, a brand new bodega making just one wine, a crisp dry white, but with a style that marks it as one of the best of the new wave wines of Spain.

Founded by businessman Ismael Manuat, who returned to his village in the hills behind Alella to revive the local winemaking tradition, Alta Alella is a small but fully computerised winery with ranks of stainless steel temperature-controlled fermenters in the modern tradition.

Manuat has spared no expense to make the wine he calls Marqués de Alella after the eponymous marqués, who has a small stake in the venture. He has planted his own neat vineyard but also buys grapes from his neighbouring farmers, uses 60 per cent Pansa Blanca and the balance Xarel-lo, takes only the free run juice from these grapes, ferments it slowly in stainless steel at a low temperature, then immediately bottles the wine to preserve its freshness. There is oak in the cellar, but it seems to slip Ismael Manuat's mind that the wine is supposed to go into it for a year. The crisp, fresh, slightly citrusy aroma, and the clean dry and fresh flavour of Marqués de Alella, show just how good such wines can be when modern winemaking is applied to local grape varieties. It has been a singular success since it first appeared in 1982.

The third winery in the region is Vinos Jaime Serra, which sells under the Alellasol label two white wines and a rosé, and the area also has its own Cava producer in Parxet, who also produce still wines. Owned by the Sunol family, and based on their 47 hectares of vineyard, Mas Parxet has been a Cava producer since 1920. They now make three good Cava wines from Parellada, Macabeo and Xarel-lo grapes grown in the Alella hills, and round off the total production of the pocket size denominacion.

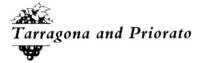

Tarragona and Priorato

Tarragona is co-operative country. In several parts of Spain the bulk of the wine produced comes from the local co-operatives, rather than private or corporate producers, and this is one bastion. It is rare for a village within the denominated grape-growing area not to have its co-operative, and some are of an impressive size. Almost all of the 6 million litres of Tarragona wine produced annually comes out of these co-operatives.

Some, like the Celler Cooperativa de Valls, the Cooperativa Agricola Falset, the Cooperativa Agricola Caja Rural or the Union Agraria Cooperativa, bottle and sell a part of the wine they make under their own names, but most sell all of their wine in bulk to shippers or importers who bottle under their own name, and a fifth of Tarragona's white wine production goes to the Cava houses up the coast for conversion to sparkling wine.

It would be wrong to think that because Tarragona is co-operative country that fundamental changes have not taken place, and are continuing to do so, in the style of Tarragona wines and how they are made. Only a few years ago, Tarragona's reputation was for heady red and dessert wines. Now, through a substantial investment in new winemaking equipment, better skills both in the wineries and the vineyards, and an awareness of what the foreign buyers want, Tarragona is rapidly becoming known for its fresh, clean white wines, and lighter, well constructed red wines.

The region may not rank amongst the great wine areas of Spain, but it is solid and dependable, producing consistent wines for daily drinking.

Like most of the coastal vineyard zones, vines reached Tarragona with the Phoenicians, and the area's reputation for wine was further enhanced by the Romans, who much appreciated it. Their long and solid presence in what they called Tarraco can still be seen in modern Tarragona, where the skyline is still dominated by the massive fortifications they built, and where the visitor can still walk in the old Roman forum.

Then and now the long warm summer days tended to produce grapes that gave strong wines, high in natural alcohol, which the Tarragonans further bolstered by fortification. To the Victorians this was poor man's port. But the world does not want such wines now, and while they continue to be made, the advent of cold fermentation has permitted the Tarragonans to move away from these centuries-old traditions.

Viticulturally Tarragona, the largest of the Catalonian denominaciones covering some 24,000 hectares, has been subdivided into three smaller regions, each different in climate and soils. Campo de Tarragona is the largest area, running along the coast on each side of the city of Tarragona and inland up to 30 kilometres. Flat land broken here and there by small ravines and mesas, and also home to thousands of hazelnut trees, for which the province is famous, its soils are decomposed limestone, and its climate mild, due to the influence of the sea. It is the best of the regions for white wines and lighter reds.

Inland, to the south of the denominacion, is Ribero de Ebro, on the banks and slopes of the valley carved by the river Ebro on its long meander from the Rioja region to the Mediterranean. Its alluvial soils and dry climate yield full bodied red and deepish whites, but with good levels of acidity.

The third area, Comarca de Falset, is in the mountainous hinterland which acts as something of a sun trap, and the vines, planted in granitic soils, give huge, inky wines, that by law must have a minimum 12 degrees alcohol, but can get up to 16 or 17 degrees on their own. Falset wine forms the backbone for many a good Spanish sangria: tourists soaking it up with the sun are in for a rough morning after.

Tarragona was granted its Denomination of Origin in 1945, one of the earlier Spanish regions to receive it, and under the current rules only certain grape varieties are permitted. For white wines they are Parellada for fresh and fruity wines, Xarel-lo for wines with body, Macabeo for crisp acidity, all three also the defined grapes for Cava wines, and Garnacha Blanca for wines with less acidity, more body. Moscatel is also grown for sweeter wines.

The red varieties are Garnacha Tinta and Garnacha Peluda, Carinena and Ull de Llebre or Tempranillo. At the research station at Reus, and in the vineyards of one or two producers, trials are also being done on the white grape Colombard, and the noble red varieties Cabernet Sauvignon, Merlot and Syrah, or Shiraz, that could add another dimension to Tarragonan wines.

At the moment the skill of the Tarragonans lies in the blending of the wines from the three sub-regions, and from the different grape varieties, to achieve consistency of style from year to year. A few, like the important producer Lopez Bertran with their single variety Macabeo and Parellada white wines, are looking in a new direction. But the vast majority of Tarragona wines will be simply labelled blanco, dry or sweet, tinto or rosado.

Alongside these wines are the survivors of the past, the sweet, fortified or unfortified wines. The best known is Tarragona clásico, still much favoured in the bars of Barcelona. Basically a clásico is a bit like an old sherry with a dash of port. It is made by holding the wine in cask, or in some instances in glass jars that are left in the sun. The wine oxidises and deepens. Some are fortified, others not, but they can reach up to 22 degrees alcohol, and the very best will be run through a solera system, the same as used for maturing sherry, to mingle with older wine and pick up more flavour and personality. They come under the general heading of rancio wines, still made for local consumption in many parts of Spain.

The other speciality of the region, and of one bodega in particular, is altar wine. De Muller, based near the harbour of Tarragona, have been supplying the popes with these wines for over a century. They are sweet, fortified Moscatel or Macabeo wines, allowed to mature in old American oak casks, developing with time a deep, raisiny flavour. Some are left to attain a venerable age.

Within the overall Tarragona region are two smaller denominaciones, Priorato, and the new Terra Alta, both in mountainous country.

Priorato wine is something of a legend amongst the Catalonians, and though it has been described as one of the classic wines of the world, it remains undiscovered. It is basically a whopping great red wine, sometimes maderised, made in the ruggedly remote, virtually unchanged mountains inland from Tarragona. The Carinena and Garnacha vines for the wine are planted on steep slopes rising up to 1,400 metres, where the soils, despite the volcanic origin of the area, are an unusual combination of red slate dotted with particles of mica which glitter in the sun. The locals all it *Llicorella*.

The area has cold winters but long, hot summers, with temperatures rising to 35 degrees Centigrade, and the added heat for the grapes of El Seré, the Mediterranean Mistral, and the warmth picked up by the mica specks in the soil. The result is a red wine that can naturally reach 18 degrees of alcohol, is virtually black when young, almost overwhelms the flavour buds, and lives to a great age. It is certainly not a wine to be trifled with.

Most Priorato is made by the local co-operatives who sell it on in bulk for commercialisation by others. De Muller bottle some, as does Scala Dei, one of the few bodegas in Spain to be run by a woman, Asuncion Peyra, who is also the local mayoress. She also makes a fine, cherry coloured rosé from Garnacha grapes, and is trying Cabernet Sauvignon and Chenin Blanc as the possible basis for new wines. Bodegas Rotllan and Rafael Barril also bottle in the region.

Terra Alta is also mountain country, yet in complete contrast its reputation is for white wines from Garnacha Blanca and Macabeo vines planted in the limestone soils of the plateaus and valleys of the area. Despite its hinterland location, Terra Alta has a Mediterranean climate, and olives are also grown in the region.

The relative warmth gives fuller bodied white wines, with the depth of flavour in the past being enhanced by maceration on the skins, or *vi brisant* as it is known locally. However, new roads have opened up the area a little, and the locals no longer have to drink most of their own wine. It has also brought a realisation that lighter, fresher wines are what the market wants, so more are being made from grapes picked earlier to generate less alcohol, and fermented *vi verge,* or off the skins. Terra Alta has only been a denominacion in its own right since 1972, but in the near future its white wines, with their distinctive perfume and flavour of almonds, will become another Spanish discovery.

For the immediate future, Tarragona will continue to do what it does best—produce decent wines at decent prices. It will not be challenging its next door neighbour Penedes for quality. But a visit to a winery like Lopez Bertran, with its serried ranks of spotless stainless steel temperature-controlled fermenters, its rows of new oak, its ultra modern bottling lines, is to see a massive

Rueda, the small village from which the wine takes its name.

Training vines on wires is rarely seen in Spain, but is becoming more frequent in the best Penedes vineyards.

The shallow Duero river valley forms a unique microclimate on the flat Castille-Leon plain.

In Rueda the poda en vaso *or bush vine system is used to shield the vine from the winds and protect grapes from the sun.*

investment in the future of the province and its wines. That technology will eventually be unleashed.

Lerida

Lerida is an outpost of Spanish viticulture, a semi-desert that has been made to bloom through the efforts of one family. When Manuel Raventos Domenech came to the arid Lerida region of Catalonia, to the north of the Penedes and virtually on the border of Aragon, he had a vision. He would build a model estate, based on agriculture, and turn the desert into a garden.

It was fortunate that he was one of the leading members of the Raventos family, who 30 years earlier had begun amassing a fortune through the introduction of their Codorniu sparkling wines, the first in Spain made by the champagne method, and now one of the major brands in the world.

Don Manuel faced a herculean task. The soils had been leached of almost all their goodness, erosion was rampant, and water unavailable, or too saline to use. Undeterrred he bought 3,300 hectares, and employed thousands of labourers to clear the scrubland, revitalise the land with tons and tons of fertiliser, minerals and other constituents, plant thousands of trees, dig miles of irrigation ditches, and sink hundreds of bores for water.

It was an enormous task. But it worked. The desert began to bloom again with pear and apple trees, vines, pasture land, vegetable fields, oranges and other fruits, and Lerida became an agricultural community in its own right.

A castle became the family home, and the estate took the name Raimat. On the arched entrance to the castle were carved a bunch of grapes and a hand, with *raim* in Catalan, meaning grapes, and *mat*, meaning hand.

In reintroducing grapes to Lerida, Don Manuel revived an old tradition, but his efforts did not meet with great viticultural success. It was left to his grandson, Daniel Pages, to turn Raimat into one of the earliest examples of modern Spanish viticulture. An eminent viticulturalist, well known within the portals of UC Davis, the great Californian wine university and research centre,

Don Daniel was determined to replant the vineyards with top quality varieties. Beginning around 1960, he instituted a programme beginning first with the best native Catalan varieties, Parellada, Macabeo, and Xarel-lo, then from 1975 made a major push into imported varieties, beginning with Cabernet Sauvignon and Chardonnay, the first really substantial plantings of these two varieties undertaken in Spain, and towards the end of the 1970s, when these two varieties had shown they would adapt to the conditions, their acreages were increased and plantings of Merlot, Pinot Noir and the native Tempranillo were begun. From 1975 onwards, all the plantings were of clonally selected, virus-free varieties imported from UC Davis, grafted onto American rootstocks.

Raimat now has about 850 hectares of vines, massive by Spanish standards, excepting Jerez, of which Cabernet Sauvignon [320 hectares] and Chardonnay [200 hectares] predominate. All the vines excepting Parellada are trained on wires in the Double Guyot system, again uncommon in Spain, where the bush vine is the norm.

The climate of Raimat, despite being 300 metres above sea level, is not a particularly hospitable one: it gets blazing hot in the summer, and the vineyards get little more than 300 mm of rainfall a year. So a lot of innovative work has had to be done to protect the vines. All the vineyards are fully established for irrigation, and apart from trickle irrigation in the spring, a series of sprinklers pop their heads above the vines. When they are turned on they can create a blanket of moist air above the vineyard, mitigating the heat of the sun's rays. Much attention has also been paid to pruning and leaf technology to also get the best out of the vines. Mechanical harvesting is used, again not normal in Spain as the bush vines elsewhere are too low.

Complementing the vineyards is an extraordinary winery, designed and built in the 1920s by a pupil of the distinguished architect Gaudi. With high vaulted ceilings, curved windows, and a great feeling of space, it is almost a cathedral to wine. It looks as if it was built a few years ago, and is architectually important as one of the first major buildings in Spain to use concrete extensively.

Within are row upon row of stainless steel fermenters, and row upon row of new oak casks to mature the best wines. No cost has been spared to match the technology in the vineyards. It handles around 6.5 million kilos of grapes each vintage, but runs as smoothly as an ocean liner.

Some of the Chardonnay wine made has been diverted into

Codorniu's top sparkling wines, with Anna de Codorniu Brut Reserva having around 15 per cent in its cepage, and a new Cava under the Raimat label, the Blanc de Blancs Brut Nature, having 85 per cent in its blend.

However, Raimat is there to produce table wines, and though there is no denominacion for the province yet (it is being considered), they are some of the better new wines of Spain, with a more cosmopolitan appeal.

The main white wine is the very good Clos Casal, a blend, in roughly equal proportions, of Chardonnay, Parellada and Macabeo, and Raimat Chardonnay, a varietal wine. The red Clos Abadia is half Cabernet Sauvignon and the balance Tempranillo, a good combination as the grapes blend well together.

Raimat, it must be said, is not making outstanding wines. Others are doing better with imported varieties. The climate and soil are the likely reasons. But to make enjoyable, middle to upper rank wines from an area that once only sustained a few goats and stringy sheep is an achievement indeed.

Ampurdan-Costa Brava

Ampurdan-Costa Brava is the most northerly of the Catalonian denominations, tucked into the lee of the Pyrenees on the very border with Mediterranean France. Like many other parts of Spain, it produces reasonable amounts of modest wine for local consumption and for sale to tourists enjoying the beaches of the coast. It would have gone unremarked except for the activities of one of the handful of producers in Ampurdan, the family company called Perelada, which figured in a court case that has entered the annals of legal history.

Perelada was, and still is, a producer of sparkling wines. However, it attempted to sell these wines through its British agents, the Costa Brava Wines Company, in bottles bearing labels using the word 'champagne'. The incensed Champenois took legal action, and the case came to court in 1960, in an action taken by some of the bigger champagne houses representing the whole industry.

After a protracted legal wrangle, judgement was given that only the Champenois had the right to the name champagne, a right that has now been recognised throughout Europe and in several other countries—though not by the United States and Australia—and which has just been extended within the EEC to the use of the descriptive term methode champenoise.

Perelada have long since embraced the Cava concept at their winery, which rather unusually is in the cellars of the imposing castle fortress of Perelada, owned by the company, which is known as Cavas del Ampurdan. Gran Claustro is the flagship of their Castillo de Perelada range of Cava wines. In the same cellar, though divided by a steel barrier to conform with the law, the same company also makes a range of table wines from the native Catalonian grapes, including the fresh young white Pescador and the red Cazador. In a third, new installation outside the castle, again to conform with the law, they make sparkling wine by the cuve close [tank] method.

Visitors to the area may also encounter table wines from the local co-operative under the Espolla name, and from the privately owned Covinosa, whose main label is Vi de L'Any, and whose red wine is recommended, as is the Vi Novell of Oliveda.

CHAPTER 5

Galicia

Galicia is a series of paradoxes. It is soft, verdant country, with abundant rainfall, that becomes a blaze of colour as its autumn hues arrive, very different from most of the rest of Spain, where the land is hard, brown and often in the grip of drought.

It has two denominated areas, but some of its best wines come from outside these areas. It has hundreds of small grape growers who make their own wine, whereas in most other regions the growers sell their grapes to a limited number of co-operatives and private bodegas. It has a bewildering plethora of grape varieties, most of them totally obscure, while other regions concentrate on just a few. It produces Spain's most expensive white wine yet also some of the dreariest white wines to be found anywhere in this large country. And it is the only region where a grape variety has been 'denominated'. It is the only part of Spain where the vines are trained on arbours to get *more* sunshine. And for good measure it is the only part of Spain that was never conquered by the Moors.

Galicia is the very north-western part of Spain, with the Atlantic to the west, the province of Leon to the east, and northern Portugal to the south. The coastline, including the famous sailor's landmark, the great lion-headed boss of Cape Finisterre, is splendidly dramatic, with deep fjords, or *rias* as they are known locally. When the rains cease the air is crisp and fragrant with the scents of pine and eucalyptus.

Crisp too is the best description for the famous *aguja* or needle wines of Galicia, wines that have been known for centuries. The red wine of Amandi was said to be a favourite of Caesar Augustus. He must have had a fair palate, because it is still the best red wine of Galicia. In 1386, John of Gaunt's army were inebriated on these wines for two days, and in the retreat from La Coruña, Sir John Moore saw his drunken soldiers cut down by the pursuing French during the Peninsular War.

Galicia's most famous city is Santiago de Compostella, where St James the Apostle died at the end of his missionary travels, and which became a magnet for pilgrims in the Middle Ages. The sign of a pilgrim was the scallop shell, from one of the many fine seafoods harvested off the Galician coast. Those travellers too found relief in the wines of Galicia at the end of their long pilgrimage.

Galicia is one of the wettest parts of western Europe, and many of its vine varieties have a strong Germanic influence, possibly brought to the region by Cluniac monks in the twelfth century, who thought those varieties would best adapt to the Galician climate. Yet the variety used to make much of the wine is the Palomino of Jerez, often referred to as *Jerez* in the region, from one of the hottest parts of Spain.

For both red and white wines, a first, second and third division is now being established for the different varieties. For the white wines, the only player in the first division is the Albariño of northern Portugal. This is the variety that has its own denominacion, a *Denominacion especifica* covering the variety, the only one of its kind in Spain. All other denominaciones cover a district, with the exception of Cava which covers a style of wine. Not unsurprisingly, the Albariño gives a wine almost identical to the Vinhos Verdes of northern Portugal, its native country.

In the second division are Triexadura, Godello, Torrontes, Loureira, Macabeo and Albilla. In the third, Palomino, or Jerez. Added to that are a host of totally obscure vine varieties like the Lado, found only in the vineyards around the tiny village of Remuino in the Arnoia district, which occasionally give a local gem of a wine.

First division red varieties are Caino, Mencia, Garnacha [also known locally as Alicante], Tempranillo and Bancellao, and in the second the likes of Souson and Ferron.

It is estimated that Galicia has around 100 different grape varieties planted, and the Albariño apart, it is a bewildering task to try to identify a regional style in its wines. Who knows what varieties are used to make this or that wine?

Even the two denominated areas are quite different, both physically and in the style of wines they produce. Valdeorras to the east, nearer to Leon, has red wines closer in style to those of Leon. The climate is Continental, though more humid than usual, the soils slaty, and the vines are bush vines, *poda en vaso*. Irrigated by the River Sil, this part of the province of Orense is far less Galician in its nature.

Valdeorras has around 5,000 hectares under vine, and its warmer disposition means its wines are higher in alcohol than the rest of the region. Though the Alicante is the most widely grown variety in the denominacion, its best wines are the red wines made from Mencia. They are cherry red in colour, fresh, fruity and aromatic, with decent body. Crianza wines are also made, but these reds are best drunk when young.

Decent examples are the Albar of the co-operativa Jesus Nazareno and the Pingadelo of the co-operativa Virgen de las Viñas, but in all honesty they are not wines to be hunted down with ruthless determination.

What is interesting is the white wine made from the Godello grape, with its strong aroma and full but fresh flavour with good fruit. They are interesting local wines, and the best are the Gran Vino Godello of Jesus Nazarino or the Brisel of Virgen de las Viñas.

Ribeiro to the west is typically Galician, rolling green hills with the vines trained high on pergolas. It is remarkably akin to the Minhao of northern Portugal where the Vinhos Verdes come from, and, like that region, its white wines are infinitely better than its reds. The climate is Atlantic, the soils granitic, but despite the verdant appearance of the countryside, rather poor. The vines are trained high to get more sunshine, and to release more land for growing other crops, like cabbages. There are about 2,700 hectares under vine, including Albariño.

A third possible denominacion, Valle de Monterrey, between the two, has been discussed but not approved, for the remarkably simple reason that no wine is bottled in this region.

Outside the two denominaciones are other growing areas, just as important, making just as good wine, including El Rosal, Cambados y Valle del Salñes, Condado del Tea, Chantada, Betanzos and Ribera del Sil.

The co-operative movement is weak in Galicia. There are only half a dozen. However there are hundreds of small grower winemakers, each doing their own thing with the varieties they have planted. In the western part the common problem they face is too much acidity and too little alcohol in their wines. A poorly made white wine in this region can be screamingly acidic to the point of being undrinkable, and most of the red wines are too tart to have any appeal.

The lack of alcohol—many wines are only around 9 degrees —also means the wines are fragile, do not travel well, and have a tendency to oxidise rather too quickly. However, lack of ability to travel is not seen as a problem by the Gallegos, as they drink virtually the whole output themselves. The Gallegos drink 134 litres of wine per head per year, and in Orense it rises to 180 litres. The average is three times that for the rest of Spain, and despite being the sixth largest wine-producing region of the country, Galicia still has to import some 60 per cent of its wine needs from other regions, and it is no secret that some wines purporting to be wholly Galician have been stretched with wine from La Mancha.

The hundreds of small producers vary in their winemaking skills and equipment. Some simply ferment the wine in any old container, then start drinking it with Galician gusto. Others are careful in their vinification techniques, and though stainless steel is rare in the region, the very best wines have seen it. So it is possible to taste both the ridiculous and the sublime in Galicia, and the restaurateurs of Spain spend days hunting down the best wines, which they will then sell at remarkably high prices.

A top Albariño fetches the highest price of all. Grown on arbours, its small sweet grapes yield a good wine, though the buyer must beware for, while the denominacion especifica says this must be wholly varietal wine, some producers are not above throwing in some lesser grapes.

The best example is not quite typical of the wine. In the non-denominated Cambados area, the Marques de Figueroa uses part of his Palacio de Fefiñanes to make his Albarino de Fefiñanes, which, unusually, he ages in oak, the younger version getting two years, the reserva six years, losing the petillance that naturally occurs in the wine, giving it a deeper colour and less greenness, and rounding it out somewhat. In sibling friendship he allows his brother, Don Joaquin Gil Armada, to make his Albariño del Palacio from his own small vineyard.

A more typical Albariño will have a light petillance, a very fresh, green aroma, sometimes with a floral hint, and a mouthwateringly acidic green flavour, with a distinct resin touch, which can also appear on the nose. The finish should be as crisp as an iceberg lettuce, but can tend to seem tart. The Castel de Fornos of Bodegas Chaves in Cambedos, the Marqués de Sernan from Salñes, generally considered to be the best area for Albariño, or the

Cooling equipment and cold fermentation stainless steel tanks have transformed the style of many Spanish wines, including the best wines of Galicia which are regarded in Spain as the country's finest white wines.

Dom Bardo of the Agrupacion Cosecheiros do Salñes, are more typical examples.

The white wines, made from a mixture of grapes, are more varied in style. The Santiago Ruiz Blanco from the bodega of the same name in the El Rosal area has a high percentage of Albariño in it, and shows a good, fruity, balanced aroma and flavour. The Pazo Blanco from the Cooperativa del Ribero has a slightly earthy, hard edge to it, while their Vina Costeira has a slightly perfumed–soap aroma and resiny flavour. This wine is Treixadura

61

and Torrontes. The clean, fresh Blanco of Campante is a third decent example, while their Tinto is one of the better reds of the region, purply plump, fresh and fruity, with a crisp acid bite at the finish. The Pazo Tinto is much the same.

The best red wine of Galicia is generally considered to come from around the village of Amandi in the Ribero del Sil. Steep plots on the banks of the Sil are planted with Mencia and Alicante, and their aspect gives a red wine with more body and alcohol than is found elsewhere in the region, though an Amandi red is still rather light and fruity.

Both red and white wines should be well chilled to keep the acidity muted, and they are best within the year of the vintage. For the white wines, anything over two years old is likely to show signs of oxidation, with the exception of Fefiñanes. A deeper orange yellow colour is a sure sign.

The Gallegos often drink their red wine from delicate porcelain cups, as they do the local spirit drink called Queimada, a Galician version of the French *marc* or Portuguese *bagaceira*. This would not be worth mentioning were it not for the charming brochure that the main producer, the Cooperativa del Ribeiro of Pazo fame, likes to issue.

Talking of their aguardiente, used as the basis for Queimada, they say:

This is one of the strongest drinks in the world, a drink which taken by itself requires three men to a glass; one to drink it, and two friends to support him.

If drunk in the form of Queimada it is transformed into a deceptively mild nectar, dangerous in the extreme by virtue of the spell it casts.

The Cooperavistas of Ribeiro recommend that before drinking it, you pin a card with your address on the lapel of your jacket.

Galician gastronomy is very much based on the harvest of the sea, crayfish, crabs, scallops, mussels, fish and the like, and its best white wines go exceedingly well with these foods. In La Coruña the wines are best tasted with the small red crabs called *necoras*, in Santiago with the scallops of St James.

Perhaps it is because the white wines, and in particular the Albariño, are so different in taste to what is found elsewhere in Spain, that a cult has grown up around them. In mid-August, the island of La Toja, off the Galician coast, hosts a Fiesta de Albariño, to which the loyal followers of the variety flock to sample the most expensive white wine in Spain.

No one makes a great fuss over the Vinhos Verdes of Portugal. They are seen as nice, fresh, inexpensive wines for day-to-day drinking. The Spanish versions are certainly no better, and in many cases much worse. They are at their best very pleasant accompaniments to the gastronomy of Galicia, but in a wider context rather overrated.

CHAPTER 6

Castille-Leon

Ribera del Duero

Rioja may consider itself the king of Spanish red wines, but there is an upstart who is rapidly developing into a serious pretender to the throne. That upstart is Ribera del Duero.

As Spanish wine lovers and wine writers have become more adventurous in their search for new Spanish wines, they have discovered the wines of Ribera again, and are writing about them very enthusiastically indeed. Yet what Ribera was and is capable of achieving has always been there, under their noses, in the wine known as Vega Sicilia, arguably Spain's greatest red table wine, and the locomotive that has pulled all the others along.

However, Vega Sicilia was Vega Sicilia, standing on its own and not particularly identified with Ribera del Duero, and it was only when other bodegas in the region were 'discovered' that Ribera became known as an area for top quality red wines in the modern context.

Riberan red wines are the brotherly half to the white wines of Rueda. Both are on the broad plateau of Castille Leon, the old Catholic heart of Spain. To the north of Madrid, both vineyard areas are oases in mile after mile of flat land where wheat and other cereals form a moving carpet of yellow gold in the summer, and there is a sense of silent timelessness.

While the vineyards of Rueda sit amid the wheatfields of this flat, historic land, Ribera del Duero has what could be described as a microclimate. The River Duero, which eventually crosses over into Portugal to become the magnificent Douro valley of port fame, here has carved a shallow river valley framed by a series of lowish hills on both sides, and fertile enough to sustain crops other than just wheat, amongst them the vine. It is still part of one of the coldest winter hinterlands of Spain and one of the hottest in the summer, but even then the night temperatures plunge dramatically.

Ribera del Duero is one of the newer denominaciones in Spain, with its Regulamento only coming into force in 1982. It is one of the smaller denominaciones, with around 12,000 hectares of vines, but manages to fall within four provinces, Soria to the east, Burgos to the north, Valladolid to the west and Segovia to the south. It is in the middle of a part of Spain steeped in history. Burgos, famous for its crenellated cathedral where in one chapel is supposed to be the preserved body of Christ, found by fishermen floating off the coast some many miles away. Avila, to the south, is ringed by its turreted battlements, Segovia has its soaring cathedral, and monumental aqueduct dating back to the time of the Roman emperor Trajan, and Valladolid, famous for its scholarship. This is the land that forged El Cid, properly known as Rodrigo Diaz de Vivar, who finally broke the Moors and became one of the greatest heroes of Spain.

The El Cid of Ribera and Spain is Vega Sicilia, and heroic is an apt description: Vega is a mighty red wine, and stands apart from its peers.

Vega Sicilia is a large *finca* [farm] of almost 1,000 hectares, given over to vines, maize, sheep, alfalfa and beets. The vineyards, covering 120 hectares, are on the lower slopes of a series of smallish hills, while the other crops are planted closer to the river on flat land. Like the rest of Ribera, the vineyard soils are a mixture of clay and sand, with limestone outcrops.

The first vines were planted in 1864 by Don Eloy Lecanda y Chaves, and the name derives from an old reference to the farm as Vega de Santa Cecilia, the latter being corrupted to Sicilia.

Don Eloy must have been a singular man, for long before the French influence spread into Spain in the wake of phylloxera, he travelled north to Bordeaux and returned with Cabernet Sauvignon, Merlot and Malbec cuttings to plant on his farm, also adding the local variety Tinto Fino, a close relative of Tempranillo.

He planted these varieties on the lower slopes of the farm, and to vintage the grapes built a red brick bodega, a series of curved arches, with, in the centre, a small private chapel, not an unusual sight in a winery in this very religious part of Spain. He also built a typical Castillian family home nearby which bears more than a passing resemblance to a French chateau.

For more than a century the family restricted the production of Vega Sicilia to a peak of around 20,000 bottles, and its reputation grew through its quality and scarcity. However, in 1983 it passed into the hands of David Alvarez Diaz, the wealthy owner of security and cleaning companies, who has transformed Vega Sicilia into a company now producing 220,000 bottles of wine a year, which will shortly be increased to 300,000 bottles.

Under the young oenologist Mariano Garcia Fernandez, the vineyards are being progressively replanted and expanded. The older vineyards, some going back 70 years, are promiscuous, with three or four varieties mixed up in each vineyard. These are being replaced by single variety vineyards. Currently the plantings are 55 per cent Tinto Fino, trained as bush vines which suit the variety better, 30 per cent Cabernet Sauvignon, trained on wires, and the balance Merlot and Malbec, with a tiny amount of the white Albillo which, with its soft flavour and high glycerine content, can enhance Vega Sicilia in a good year.

There is already a second chai in the vineyards, but the original winery has just been extended in harmony with the original building, to provide more space for bottle maturation, which Mariano Garcia sees as a new step in the evolution of Vega Sicilia.

The increased production does not mean there will be a lot more Vega Sicilia available, for although the vineyards produce just one wine, a red wine, it comes in three styles. The youngest is Vina Valbuena 3° ano, then Vina Albuena 5° ano, and finally Vega Sicilia itself, the two younger wines allowing the company to commercialise part of its production in advance of Vega Sicilia, and hence maintain its cash flow. With the 1973 Vega Sicilia for example not released until 1987, a considerable amount of capital is tied up in the evolution of the wine.

The style of Vega Sicilia very much depends on the quality of the grapes at the time of the harvest. In the worst years, like 1971 and 1978, the top wine is simply not made. In years when the weather is hot, the first fermentation is done in stainless steel. In cold years it will be done in resin-lined cement vats, and then transferred to large American oak *tinas* for the second fermentation.

In some years, when one of the principal varieties has not done so well, the different varieties will be vinified separately and a *coupage* [blend] made later. In good years all the grapes are vinified together.

In wet years, when the grapes have not picked up much natural tannin, the new wine will go into French Limousin casks. In good years, when less wood tannin is needed, the wine will go into American oak which has already been used once.

The length of time the wine spends in oak and bottle also varies according to the vintage, but a typical Vega Sicilia would spend two years in *tinas*, then two years in 600-litre casks, and finally another four to six years in new and used 225 litre barriques. The balance of its pre-release life, five years or more, is spent in bottle.

The thinking behind Vega Sicilia is, according to Mariano Garcia, to get a wine that will last at least 20 years in bottle, and in the great years like 1970, 1981 and 1982, a great deal longer.

With the two Valbuenas, the aim is to have wines that will last between eight and ten years, with the 3° anos receiving 18 months bottle maturation before release, the 5° anos two years and, naturally, having the two extra years in oak. The Valbuenas are, in effect, young Vega Sicilias, though one would suspect they are the lesser cuvees. In a good year they would represent 60 per cent of the wine made, while the balance goes on to become Vega Sicilia.

With a microclimate which means that in a good year the harvest will begin in late September, and in a difficult year, like 1984, not until 20 November, and with major divergences in the winemaking and maturation pattern, each vintage of Valbuena and Vega Sicilia is unique to an extent not often found in the wine world.

However, a typical Valbuena will have a rich purple colour, a rich, sweet, almost porty aroma with some wood showing, though quite smooth. The flavour will be full, firm, with plenty of body, spine from the oak, and good sweet ripe fruit, with a long, firm aftertaste.

A good Vega Sicilia will have a mature red brown colour, a

rich, slightly porty, complex, cedary aroma, elegant in its style, and a deep, attractive, firm, balanced, complex flavour with a character of its own. Both wines definitely need to go into the cellar for several more years.

Jan Read recounts an amusing if untrue story about Vega Sicilia. When Prince Charles was to marry Princess Diana, the Queen asked the bodega if she could have some Vega for the wedding party. 'We can let you have two cases', came the reply.

A second bodega that makes only one red wine that has been attracting much recent press coverage is that belonging to Alejandro Fernandez and his family. This unassuming man produces a wine called Pesquera at his modest winery, more a succession of sheds suitable for housing agricultural equipment than anything else.

Alejandro Fernandez found himself the centre of attention when the American wine pundit Robert Parker compared Pesquera to the mighty Chateau Petrus of Bordeaux, one of the world's most expensive red wines. This is patently ridiculous. Pesquera would not even stand up to a top red from California, say a Heitz, or a top red from Australia, let alone Chateau Petrus. However, in the Spanish context, Pesquera is a very good wine indeed, and another reason why Ribera is attracting so much interest.

Thanks to the publicity, Alejandro Fernandez has found Pesquera much in demand, and has been expanding his capacity. In 1978 he had only 10 hectares of vineyard, now he has 60, is planting more, and also buys in some wine, to give him an annual production of 300,000 bottles.

The main grape used to make Pesquera is Tinto Fino, with a small amount of Garnacha, and a tiny amount of the white Albillo. Fernandez ferments these grapes in stainless steel, at very low temperatures, but what makes his wine different is that he leaves the juice in contact with the skins for 25 days, when most wineries would only leave the skins there for that number of hours.

The wine is then left to settle for four to five months, then goes into new American oak or Limousin casks, in which Alejandro Fernandez has made a massive investment for such a small winery. The standard Pesquera gets about two years in oak and another six months in bottle before release, while the reserva wines get three years in wood and one in bottle.

Tasting the 1986 Pesquera from cask, thought to be the best vintage so far, the overwhelming impression was of a massive,

The Disneyland castle of Penafiel. Hewn from the rock on which it stands are the cellars of the best local co-operativa.

Autumn in Rueda, a brief respite before a long, freezing winter grips the plain, to be followed by a searing summer.

The famous windmills of Don Quixote dominate the skyline in parts of La Mancha, and visitors can follow his travels through this vineyard land.

mouth puckering amount of tannin masking all the other flavours. However, quite remarkably, the 1985 Pesquera, also tasted from cask at the same time, which Sr Fernandez said had been much the same a year before as the 1986, showed none of this overpowering tannin grip. It had fallen away.

The 1982 Pesquera Reserva showed the true evolution of the wine. The colour was deep with a touch of mature brown, the aroma soft, spicy, with the hard tannins gone and a slight sweetness starting to emerge. On the palate an unusual combination of flavours, a bouquet garni complexity, revealed themselves over a firm, dry, character-filled background.

The evolution of Pesquera into a very individualistic wine is most interesting, and while it may not be Chateau Petrus, it is certainly one of the best of the new wines of Spain.

Other bodegas in Ribera are not so single minded as Vega Sicilia and Pesquera, and produce a modest range of wines. Perez Pascuas is a small, spotless privately owned bodega which produces wines under the Vina Pedrosa name. It has its own 35 hectares of vineyards, and is planting more to become self-sufficient in grapes.

Again its wines are based on the Tinto Fino, or as it is called locally, Tinta del País. The owners have experimented with Cabernet and Merlot, but are not particularly happy with the results, so are basically sticking to the variety they know best.

Their range of wines is typical of Ribera, beginning with a Rosado [rosé wines are also permitted under the denominacion, but not white wines], a bone dry, almost salty wine. Then comes a Vino Joven, young, purply, fresh and fruity, a kind of local Beaujolais. Next a wood-aged crianza red, quite young, soft and fruity and easy to drink, but with underlying body, rising to the reserva red, again quite remarkably fresh and fruity, lightly sweet, with some underlying tannin, but not really revealing its age despite being around six years old on release. Cold fermentation and used oak are probably the reasons why, but in many ways these are the characteristics of a typical red from Ribera.

Other factors that influence the wines of Ribera are the relatively high altitude of the vineyards, the quite high acid levels in the soils, and the use of a little white Albillo grape juice in some wines. But this combination adds up to an attractive freshness in many of the red wines.

This characteristic is again found in the wines of the privately-owned Bodegas Penalba Lopez, whose Rosado is bone dry and

Efficient modern crushers are now in use in the majority of Spanish wineries.

fresh. Interestingly, these Ribera rosés are usually referred to as *clarete* or *claro* reds, which is rather confusing as to all intents and purposes they are a fuller-bodied style of rosé.

All the Penalba Lopez wines are sold under the name Torremilanos in Spain, after the village where the bodega is located. Again they are based on Tinto Fino or Tinta del País. The unaged tinto is fresh, fruity and slightly sweet, and the same sweetness runs through the Torremilanos crianza and reserva reds. It was explained that the Tinto Fino in Ribera has developed this characteristic sweetness, unlike its close cousin the Tempranillo of Rioja, and the sweetness could be tasted in the grapes on the vine.

The pinnacle of the Torremilanos range is their Reserva Especial, which again belies its decade of maturation to show a perfumed aroma and ripe, soft, lightly sweet flavour. As a wine exemplifying a top Ribera red, this is a better choice than the atypical Vega Sicilia or Pesquera.

Ribera del Duero is not just populated by private producers. The co-operative movement is also strong here, and making good wines. The best of them is the Co-operative Ribera Duero which has its cellars carved into the rock on which sits the snowy white Walt Disney castle of Penafiel.

Its 230 members have invested considerable sums in building new cellars, with modern vinification equipment, and cellars for its oak barrels hewn out of the mount of Penafiel, a task that must have been dirty and arduous.

The co-operative produces three range of wines, in ascending order of quality—the Ribera Duero, Penafiel and Protos ranges—with the latter wines showing a little more dryness and astringency, but otherwise being typical of the region.

Other private producers bottling the wine of Ribera are Ismael Arroyo, Victor Balbas and Vinos Garcia. The other co-operatives are Virgen de la Vega, Santisima Trinidad, Virgen de la Asuncion, Santa Eulalia, Virgen de las Vinas and San Jose Obrero.

The wines of Ribera del Duero are now in the spotlight, and deserve to be there. They represent some of the best new wines of Spain.

Rueda

The Castillian meseta to the north of Madrid reeks of Spanish history, but to the casual visitor it is mostly bleak and featureless, a place to pass through en route to the charms of Spain further south. This plateau, the highest in western Europe, bakes in the summer and freezes in the winter. Its farmers lead a hard life, a struggle against the seasons and the land to make a meagre living. With Madrid so close, it is a struggle that the younger generation are abandoning.

Valladolid, just 125 miles north of Madrid, has been the seat of the Catholic kings on more than one occasion. It was the birthplace of Philip II, the Spanish capital under Philip III, the final resting place of Christopher Colombus, the home of Cervantes, and the birthplace of the playwright José Zorilla.

At nearby Tordesillas, the Borgia Pope Alexander VI divided the New World between Spain and Portugal in 1494, and at Medina del Campo, Queen Isabel died in 1504, forbidding her ladies in waiting to uncover her feet.

With so much history, it is no surprise that the winemakers of the high plateau enjoyed a Golden Age in the sixteenth and seventeenth centuries when they supplied the Catholic court and the inns of old Madrid with wine. Gradually its influence waned, and when phylloxera struck, the vineyards were devastated. For most of the twentieth century its production was for local consumption, and not particularly good wine at that. The farmers had no money for the fancy trimmings of winemaking.

Now there is a minor revival taking place, led by a handful of bodegas, and Old Castille is finding a wider audience for some of its wines.

The white wine capital of Old Castille is Rueda, to the south of Valladolid around the farming villlages of Rueda itself, La Seca, Serrada and Nava del Rey, where tractors are just as common in the streets as cars. The low stone and brick houses of the villages are solidly built to resist the biting winter winds.

The wines of Rueda would still be largely unnoticed if it had not been for the arrival of two Marqueses in the area, the bodega Marques de Riscal, one of the leading Riojan bodegas, and the Toledo wine producer the Marques de Griñon, and the granting of the Denominacion de Origen to Rueda for its white wines in 1980.

Despite the new and well-received white wines starting to come out of the Rioja, Riscal decided the future lay in Rueda and began building an ultra modern winery, the likes of which the locals had never seen. Their first crush in 1972 was made with grapes bought from the local farmers, and it was the first release from the winery. Now the winery has built up substantial vineyards of its own, and is second only to the local co-operative La Seca in terms of production.

No expense has been spared at Riscal for the winery. High technology, with banks of stainless steel cold fermenters and storage tanks, the most modern in presses and bottling facilities, has geared the winery to the manufacture of fresh, crisp young white wine. However, things have not quite turned out as Riscal planned. Beneath the winery floor is their cellar, where once they envisaged 4,000 *barricas* would be neatly laid out to wood mature new white wines. There are *barricas*, but not in the numbers envisaged, and Riscal's expectations have not been met.

Horizontal wooden presses are now being replaced by more modern versions which extract the grape juice gently.

What Riscal did, in common with the more technically advanced wineries of Rueda, was to put their faith in the rising star grape variety Verdejo. For many years the backbone of Rueda wines was the inferior Palomino Fino, a higher yielding variety well suited to making the *generoso* and *dorado* wines for which the region was known. The shy-bearing Verdejo was hardly planted. Fortunately Riscal, and the Castillian government through the local Consejo, realised that Verdejo was the variety of the future.

The immediate plan is to replace as much Palomino with Verdejo as possible. The farmers cannot plant the other decent variety of Rueda, the Viura variety, unless their vineyards already contain more than 50 per cent Verdejo. But more importantly they are coming to realise that they will get a much better price for Verdejo than Palomino, while the costs of working their vineyards remain the same. The target is for 2,000 hectares, about half the plantings in the denominacion, to be Verdejo, and the target is well on the way to being met.

73

New rules specify that a wine of Rueda origin must have at least 25 per cent Verdejo in its make-up, with an alcohol degree of between 11.5 and 14, and to call itself Superior it must have 60 per cent Verdejo in its composition, have been aged for at least six months in oak and another six months in bottle, and have passed examination by a local tasting panel.

This is all very well, but Verdejo is a delicate grape, responding badly to having its sugar content forced to 11.5 degrees potential alcohol, and certainly having the stuffing knocked out of it for anything higher. Moreover, it is not the sort of wine that takes to wood maturation, as Riscal have found. Also there is the old question of what sort of wood? Old casks which give nothing to the wine, and in this instance are probably the better for it, or new small casks where the wood flavours are picked up far more quickly to a level where the fruit flavours of Verdejo would be submersed?

It is early days yet, and perhaps the producers and the Consejo will see that if they lower the minimal alcohol requirements, and drop the wood and bottle maturation elements as obligatory, they will get a lighter, fresher, younger wine with more youthful charm—the sort of wine that sells on the modern market.

Riscal have seen this, for they have introduced a new element to the equation. They have brought the Sauvignon Blanc to Rueda, and after initial tests have received the full blessing of the Consejo to plant this grape and as a result are creating a substantial vineyard. They are also experimenting with other varieties including Chardonnay, Rhine Riesling and Pinot Gris, and the Spanish varieties Ribero Blanco, Albariño and the Galician grape Treixadura. If they prove themselves they could be used in conjunction with Verdejo and Viura to create new and better blends, or be released as varietals as Riscal's Sauvignon Blanc has.

The Marques de Riscal white is currently about 70 per cent Verdejo, the balance Viura, and it has the crisp leafiness of a modern young wine. Their two new wines are the Sauvignon Blanc, still not quite up to scratch as the vines are still very young, but creditable wine already, and Reserva Limousin, pure Verdejo. Both are given a tickle of wood, and intelligent use of oak has certainly worked in the case of the Reserva Limousin.

Riscal's activities can certainly be acknowledged in earning Rueda its denomination, but other bodegas have not sat back and watched, they have joined in. The Marques de Griñon, who produces a superior Cabernet Sauvignon from his estate outside Toledo, also opted for Rueda to produce a partnering white wine.

At the winery owned by Antonio Sanz, he buys in grapes and uses their equipment to make a second very fresh white wine in the new style. It has not yet matched Riscal's, but it is not far away from it either.

Carlos Falco, the Marques de Griñon, now feels that while he has achieved all he can with Verdejo, it leaves his white wine somewhat one-dimensional, and he is now thinking of planting some Chardonnay in Rueda to blend into his wine to give it added complexity. It will be most interesting to see such a wine when it eventually emerges.

The other members of the Sanz family have their own bodega next door, and are following the lead of the Marques. They are also making passable Cava wines for local sale.

Another major investment in Rueda has been made by the bodega of Enrique Alvarez, where massive spending in new equipment has lifted Alvarez into third place in volume production. Using equipment developed by the beer industry, but adapted for his needs, the bodega has banks of new computer-controlled cold fermentation systems to make its new-style white wines.

The main Alvarez wine is the fresh, slightly sweet Mantel Blanco, but his most interesting wine is Mantel Nuevo Vino Ecologico, made with the minimum use of sulphur dioxide, but not quite as ecological as it sounds. The Castilla la Vieja from the bodega of the same name is another good Verdejo white.

Despite these modern influences, Rueda is still dominated by the co-operative La Seca, founded in 1935, with 400 members owning a total of 2,000 hectares of vines. Although it has introduced cold fermentation to make its Veliterra and Cuatro Rayas Rueda Superior white wines, La Seca is limited by the need to take what its members grow, and these two wines are really only reasonable everyday wines, with the Cuatro Rayas hardened by too much alcohol.

La Seca is, however, the best place to find the vinos generosos of Rueda, wines that have been made there for centuries and are still very popular locally. They have an affinity with sherry, and the locals claim they are much older than sherry as they were made when Jerez was under Moorish occupation, and wine production ceased there.

There are two types, the lighter, younger Palido, and the fuller, older, drier Dorado. A very rough equivalent would be with a full bodied fino and an older amontillado sherry, but certainly without the quality of Jerez.

A speciality of Rueda is rancio wine, a style of dessert wine made by leaving it outdoors in the summer to bake in glass jars.

Both Palido and Dorado wines are affected by flor, in the same way as sherry, after fermentation, and both are made from the Palomino Fino grape. The cheaper, rougher ones are matured in 16-litre turquoise glass rotund jars called *bombas*. These are left outside in the summer when the temperature rises to 35 degrees Centigrade during the day, and they are baked and slowly concentrated. They are then finished off in large old wood containers called *bocoyes*. These wines are sold in bulk locally.

The better generosos go through a solera system to give them a smoother, rounder character, and are sold in bottle. They range from 13 to 17 degrees alcohol in strength, with the higher strength examples having some fortification.

The Palidos and Dorados are slowly disappearing as the Ruedans turn to drinking their own fresh new white wines. The symbol of the Cosejo is a wheel [*una rueda* in Spanish] and with Riscal and others with their shoulder to the wheel it is turning towards the future. Rueda as a white wine denomination has not yet got it quite right, but it is heading in the right direction.

Leon

The traveller crossing the province of Leon at the height of the summer scans the baked ochre landscape under a relentless blue sky for the next small village where the cool interior of the tiny cantina will shut out the glare, and provide a cold drink before the next stage of the journey. Some would see this ancient landscape as desolately majestic, most as a place to pass through quickly.

It is not a tourist area, and the cathedral city of Leon is rarely disturbed by caravan convoys from the north. Yet the traveller breaking his journey in Leon can enjoy the luxury of the splendid Hotel San Marcos, once a monastery, and now a remarkable find in such a small but once so important city.

The travel writer Cedric Salter, writing in 1967, said of it:

It is precisely at the sunset hour that Leon, the ancient and dreaming city, is at its enchanted best. Perhaps the softer light hides the scars of poverty, even as candle-light conceals the wrinkles in the face of an ageing beauty, but, whatever the reason, it is the right hour in which to see Leon. The pure Gothic lines of its immense thirteenth century cathedral soar above the stained houses and the bare plateau that surrounds it, and recall that this forgotten city played a mighty part in the history of a nation.

Salter would find little changed, and it is Leon's distance from the major markets, and its burning summer climate, that explain why its wines are almost wholly for local consumption.

In the best areas for growing grapes, Valdevimbre and Los Oteros, can still be seen the curious subterranean bodegas of the local growers, tunnelled into the earth, roofed, and with the excavated dirt piled on top. Jan Read in his *Wines of Spain* aptly described them as resembling 'a giant ant-heap or prehistoric earthwork'. It would be stupid to expect anything but *corriente* [ordinary] wine to come out of them. Nor for wine buyers to look elsewhere. This wine is for consumption in homes and cantinas.

It is also, understandably, red wine that comes from the grape that dominates Leon, the Prieto Picudo, wine that can be made without the use of cold fermentation techniques. They are deep, almost jammy wines of no distinction. Prieto Picudo is also the basis of Leon's speciality, the *vinos de aguja* or needle wines. After the first fermentation, whole bunches of grapes are added to the must, triggering off further fermentation, resulting in a bone dry wine with a slight prickle to it. Served chilled, it goes well with lunch in Leon on a hot summer's day. The wine is closest to a rosé style, but not quite a traditional one.

Other red grapes are grown—Tempranillo, Garnacha and Tinta Fina—but only in limited quantities, and some white wine is made from Viura, Verdejo and Palomino.

The only producer of any substance in the region is the Planta de Elaboracion y Embotellado de Vinos, who, because their name is such a mouthful, have contracted it to the initials VILE, surely the most inappropriate name for a wine company anywhere in the world. Founded in 1966 by a group of Leon wine wholesalers, VILE now has a modern winery at Armunia, with temperature-controlled, resin-lined cement fermenters, and a good stock of oak for maturing its better red wines. VILE's Palacio de Leon white wine, made only from the Verdejo grape, is full flavoured in the mouth, but still the best white wine of Leon. Their Vina Coyanza rosé and clarete wines are fresh and youthful, showing the advantages of temperature control during fermentation, while their Don Suero six-year-old red, made from Prieto Picudo matured in American oak, is a good, inexpensive red that will continue to mature in bottle. VILE have now started to export limited quantities of these wines.

Their main rivals locally are the Bodegas La Seca, owned by a cider producer, whose main wines are Vina Guzman red, white and rosé, and their prestige red wine La Seca Reserva. The traveller can also look for the San Tirso wines from the Co-operative at Valdevimbre, and two wines from the vineyards of La Bierzo, to the north of Leon, the clarete Casa de Valdaiga, and the deeper Palacio de Arganza.

The wine trade will not be knocking on the doors of Leon, but perhaps the locals are happy to leave it that way, and let the past remain with them.

CHAPTER 7

Castille- La Mancha

La Mancha

La Mancha is the vast *meseta* or plateau of southern central Spain. Viticulturally it defies description. Mile upon mile of vineyards are broken by small olive groves, sometimes the two together, with three rows of vines to each one of olive trees, and fields of cereals. The only relief from this endless, monotonous landscape, which can stultify the brain, are the small villages, which Jan Read has aptly described as 'a row of sun-baked white houses, lining a dusty road, and dominated by the crouching bulk of its church'.

This vast, flat, timeless landscape, a perfect counter to the other Castille, Castille-Leon, is one of the largest vineyard areas in the world. It covers four Spanish provinces, and has no less than 720,000 hectares under vine, including the core zone of 120,000 hectares which come under the denominacion La Mancha. To put that in perspective, the San Joaquin Valley in California, west of Lodi, has only 220,000 hectares of vines, and a heavy proportion of the grapes are for the table, or drying into raisins.

In La Mancha the grapes are there to make wine, wine for drinking, strong wine for distilling into brandy, even wine for conversion into vinegar.

The vast output of La Mancha and Valencian wineries means the bottling line is a key piece of equipment.

Little wonder then that La Mancha may be as dry as a bone in the summer, but it is the wine lake of Spain. And with the white grape Airen accounting for 90 per cent and upwards of the vineyards planted, it has been suggested that Airen is the world's most planted grape variety, thanks to La Mancha and its offshoot Valdepenas, though logic suggests that Cabernet Sauvignon should hold the title.

In an average year, La Mancha produces a third of the total Spanish wine output, and Spain is one of the largest producers in the world. In years when yields in the north are low, this can rise to half the total Spanish production. No wonder that the EEC authorities, faced with a region that is vast in size, produces so much wine, and virtually from a single grape variety, are wondering what on earth to do about La Mancha. One suggestion is that it should be broken up into smaller denominaciones, but that still does not solve the problem of a region that is so totally outside the concepts of normal EEC wine thinking.

La Mancha is, of course, Don Quixote country. He must have been inspired to tilt at windmills out of sheer boredom with the terrain, and those windmills can still be seen in La Mancha. At the village of Consuegra there is a prime target. A low ridge runs behind the village, capped by a crumbling castle. Along the spine of the ridge are no fewer than nine whitewashed windmills, which must have given Don Quixote good sport.

Consuegra is also the home of one of La Mancha's other famous products, the most expensive herb or spice in the world—saffron. For just two weeks in November the saffron crocus flowers cover the hard La Mancha fields with a delicate lilac mantle. The flowers must be picked just as they bloom, and for hour after relentless hour the pickers stoop to pluck the fragile flowers from the soil.

Each saffron flower has three stigmas, orange hued, and they must be delicately removed from the flowers by the skilled fingers of the village women, for they are what become, when dried, the saffron spice. It takes between 200,000 and 400,000 stigmas to make just one pound of saffron, which it why it has been compared to gold.

La Mancha does not have a wine route, but it has a Don Quixote route, and visitors can follow his trail from village to village, where much of what Cervantes wrote still holds true today. The region is dotted with Don Quixote bars, Cervantes restaurants and Sancho Panza souvenir stalls. The quixotic knight has even been adopted as the logo for the La Mancha seal of guarantee for its wines of denominacion.

In a way this is appropriate, as the grape growers have their own windmills to tilt at: how to make better wine in a region with a relentless, often drought-stricken climate, a climate described as nine months of winter, three months of hell, that is dominated by one grape variety, and not a particularly good one at that. Their only solution so far has been the introduction of cold fermentation in stainless steel to put more life into the white La Mancha wine, but at best it remains day-to-day wine, *vino corriente*, and because there is so much of it, prices are relatively low and supplies guaranteed, which attracts the big supermarket buyers from all over Europe like moths to a candle.

The denominacion of La Mancha, the core of the region, lies

within the provinces of Toledo, Ciudad Real, Cuenca and Albacete. It has 120,000 hectares under vine, mainly owned by small growers who have, on average, 12 hectares each. In a normal year the combined production of denominacion wine is about 3 million hectolitres, made by some 160 co-operatives and private bodegas. In the biggest, the scale of winemaking is monolithic, with vast stainless steel or resin-lined cement tanks to ferment and hold the wine. Here winemaking is a military operation.

Airen has had a stranglehold on La Mancha for more than three centuries. It is trained close to the ground, *en cabeza*, or head shaped, to preserve any moisture and protect the grapes from the summer sun. Airen is a hardy variety that has adapted to the local conditions, which is why the growers like it. They are frightened that if they introduce other, better varieties, they will not be able to handle the severe conditions. So most of the research being done at the viticultural station at Alcazar de San Juan is on how to improve the Airen.

Currently it gives low yields, around three kilos of grapes per vine, or between 25 and 28 hectolitres per hectare. The very dry conditions of the region keep the yields low, but also mean the vineyards are remarkably free of diseases, and the La Mancha grower only has to deal with pruning and harvesting in the course of his viticultural year.

Spain does not permit irrigation in its vineyards, which is just as well. The thought that the La Mancha vineyards could be irrigated and yields doubled would give any wine administrator nightmares. Europe would be awash with wine.

Airen accounts for 90 per cent of all the vines planted, whereas half a century ago the other main variety of the region, the red Cencibel, was more widely planted than it is today. However, it is more fragile than Airen, and to protect their livelihoods, many growers switched from the red to the white variety. Now, with the help of EEC subsidies, the Consejo Regulador is hoping some growers will plant more Cencibel once again.

The main change in the Airen wine of La Mancha was more or less forced on the producers at the beginning of the decade when the big supermarket buyers of Britain told their suppliers that unless the Spanish made better wines they would take their custom elsewhere.

One of those big suppliers, Rodriguez & Berger, responded by introducing the first wines made by cold fermentation in 1983. Now just over half the wine of denominacion is made this way. There has been other fine tuning in the shape of earlier picking to

In La Mancha, not all the co-operatives have been able to embrace new technology, and it shows in some of the wines.

get higher acidity and lower alcohol degree, lighter pressing, earlier bottling, and with a reduction of fermentation temperatures by something like 10° Centigrade, to around 18°, a new generation of Airen white wines is being made.

The difference between a traditional La Mancha wine and a new wave one is quite obvious in terms of colour, aroma and flavour. The traditional wine will be made from grapes picked at the beginning of October by growers who are paid by alcohol degree. The grapes will be pressed to get all the juice out of them, and the juice will be fermented in open earthenware *tinaja* jars together with the skins. The wine is traditionally not sold until the third year after the harvest.

It will have a dark lemon colour, a dull, flat, somewhat earthy aroma, a neutral, somewhat cooked flavour and an alcohol degree of 13–14. It is prone to oxidation at an early age, and is really only suitable for blending away, but much of it is still sold by the glass for a handful of pesetas in the bars of Spain.

Grapes for the new white wines will be picked around mid-September, the growers will be paid a premium for acidity/alcohol balance, the grapes will be pressed gently in modern horizontal presses, and only the free run and first pressing juices used. The must will then be cold fermented in stainless steel or resin-lined cement tanks, and bottled quickly to preserve freshness.

The result is pale white wines, with a light, fresh, floral, clean aroma and a bone dry, clean flavour and an alcohol degree of between 11 and 12.5. They are not great wines by any standards, but are a vast improvement on the white wines of just a few years ago.

There is little variation in style or quality from one bodega to the next, for they are all working with the same variety using the same techniques, and in a region where the climate may be harsh, but is also relatively stable from year to year. So a white or red La Mancha wine, or a red or white Valdepenas wine from a similar and adjoining denominacion, will be much the same from vintage to vintage, which is another reason why they are attractive to supermarket buyers.

Some rosado wines are made in La Mancha by blending some Cencibel juice with Airen to give wines with a pale onion-skin colour, a dry, fresh aroma, and a lightly fruity flavour with a clean finish.

The red wines made from Cencibel will either be released young, when they are fresh and fruity with a crispness from the acidity, or will be given some exposure to oak where they will firm up and become a little drier. The *crianza* wines must have at least one year in oak, and be a minimum of two years old before release, and the best of both styles are quite acceptable reds in a humble way.

The Airen and Cencibel are not the only varieties permitted under the La Mancha denominacion. The white varieties Pardella, Macabeo and Verdoncho, and the red Garnacha Tinta and Moravia are also allowed, though in practice they are scarce. However, at the viticultural research station, experiments are taking place with an interesting selection of varieties: the white Parellada and Xarel-lo of Penedes, the white Pedro Ximinez of Montilla, the white Viura of the Rioja and Navarra, the red grape imports Cabernet Sauvignon, Merlot and Syrah, the Sumoll and Monastrell of Penedes, and the Prieto Picudo of Leon.

So far, the Cabernet Sauvignon has shown it is ready to adapt itself to La Mancha, producing good acidity levels, but as the region is known for wines for immediate drinking, it will be difficult to persuade the growers to take on Cabernet.

At the privately-owned bodega Vinicola de Castilla, once part of the Rumasa group, twelve hectares of Cabernet have been planted, and is used to make their flagship Senorio de Guadianeja Gran Reserva, a wine that gets three years in American oak barrels. It takes on a rooftile red colour, a quite full, slightly oaky, lightly sweet aroma, and a firm dry flavour, with a hot country touch to it. What is missing is the Cabernet varietal character, but again it is an attempt to make something more of the wines of La Mancha.

In the foreseeable future, La Mancha will continue to produce a sea of wine, a vast amount of which will disappear, anonymously, into blended wines, into the bars of Spain as *vino corriente*, into the stills as the basis for Spanish brandy, or even be turned into wine vinegar.

A lot of the better wine will be tailor-made for the supermarket buyers from around the world, and be sold by those supermarkets under their own brand names. So, for example, at Rodriguez & Berger, a customer can have an off-the-shelf selection of white wines ranging from bone dry up to sweet, with a residual sugar content of 60 grammes/litre.

The leading wineries and co-operatives will also continue to offer wines under their own brand names to help the identity of La Mancha. Change will only come slowly to this vast hinterland, but even in the Spanish wine lake, changes have already been made.

Valdepenas

Valdepenas is the southern spur of the vast hinterland plateau of Castille-La Mancha, a series of small plains whose monotony is relieved by low sierras, those of Peral, Prieta and Cristo. It is dominated by the enormous La Mancha denominacion to the north, to which Valdepenas has a strong physical and climatic affinity.

Pensioned off, an old hand press now decorates a Valdepenas winery.

Both have bitter winters and scorching summers. Both suffer from lack of water, and drought is not uncommon. Both produce three main crops: wheat, olives and grapes. Both are dominated by one grape variety, the hardy white Airen.

However, Valdepenas has long been famous for its red wine, rather than white, formerly a light wine, a clarete, that was known in the past in the bars of Madrid as *aloque*, a word denoting the 'happiness' the wine brought to its imbibers. Though this term is no longer used, the reputation of Valdepenas red wines gained the area its own denominacion, and enabled it to survive in the vastness of La Mancha.

The unprepossessing, virtually unspoilt town of Valdepenas, in the centre of the denominacion, takes its name from *Val de Penas* or Valley of Stones. It was founded by the Romans, and alternated between Moorish and Catholic rule until the Reconquest was completed. Though phylloxera reached Valdepenas in 1911, the town was bursting at the seams with so much wine that trading continued while the new vineyards were established.

Today the main road into Valdepenas is wall to wall with bodegas. In the centre of the town are the oldest establishments, and on the outskirts the modern bodegas satisfying the demand for Valdepenas wine. They jostle for space with the bodegas producing a quite different product, the famous Manchego cheese, which is popular throughout Spain.

All in all there are more than 350 bodegas producing Valdepenas wine, and most are based in the town. It is a tightly-knit community largely dependent on agriculture for its livelihood, and given the harshness of the land it is no wonder that Valdepenas displays little of the affluence of other wine towns like Logrono in the Rioja.

In recent years a handful of bodegas have worked hard to lift the quality and image of Valdepenas wines beyond the carafe level. However, the region remains to a large extent a bulk wine supplier. Of the 350 odd bodegas, only 48 bottle wine, and only 18 export.

Those bodegas trying to improve quality have had to do it through the introduction of modern winemaking and maturation techniques, as the region, like La Mancha, is held in thrall by the Airen grape. In Valdepenas it accounts for 85 per cent of all plantings, the balance being the red Cencibel [the Tempranillo of Rioja]; while the local Consejo has decreed that all new and replantings must be Cencibel, and the acreage of this variety is rising, it still leaves the bodegas in an area recognised for its red wines with a problem.

In the past, in the days before Spain had wine regulations, this problem was easily solved. The bodegas simply made their white and red wines, and blended them together to make their clarete or aloque wines, young, fresh and fruity wines that could be anything from a strong bodied rosé to a young red wine. The presence of the white juice in the wine was what gave it its freshness, and hence its popularity in the bars of Madrid. As Spain neared entry into the European Economic Community, it became clear that the EEC would not permit this local habit to continue. However, under EEC rules it was possible to blend red and white must *before* vinification with the Cencibel at least 20 per cent, rising to 50 per cent, and that is how the wines are made today.

Yet this is just a temporary compromise as the balance between white Airen and red Cencibel grapes used is out of kilter with EEC practice. Before 1992, and Spain's full entry into the EEC, the whole future of the best-known wine of Valdepenas will have to be rethought.

The local producers are fortunate that the head of their Consejo is the formidable oenologist Isabel Mijares, the only woman to head a consejo in Spain, and under her guidance a solution should be found. Meanwhile a handful of the best bodegas are putting their faith in better quality fuller bodied tinto reds, enhanced with oak maturation.

The flat plains of Valdepenas are planted with 35,000 hectares of vines, of which 31,000 are Airen. A patch of low bush vines here, a patch there, is the rule, as there are 25,000 growers in the denominacion, over half owning less than a hectare of vines. Rarely is a vineyard more than 50 hectares.

Not unnaturally, the co-operative movement is strong, while the private bodegas find it easier to buy grapes from small growers or wine from the co-operatives than to have their own vineyards. The co-operatives have very much taken the line that they will make the wine and the private bodegas can mature it, bottle it and market it. Only one co-operative in Valdepenas, La Invencible on the old road into town, bottles some of its own wine.

The scale of the biggest bodegas, Felix Solis, los Llanos or Luis Megia, can be quite intimidating. It is not unusual to see stainless steel fermenters or holding tanks of a million litres capacity, and at Luis Megia, for example, they can crush up to a million kilogrammes of grapes a day. This is a scale of production not often seen outside the biggest wineries of France, California and Australia.

Yet even the most advanced bodegas still cling to the old habit of using *tinajas*, the unique, earthenware, amphorae-shaped Ali Baba jars that are also found in La Mancha, and in Montilla for making a quite different wine.

These tinajas, shaped from clay dug at Villarrobledo in La Mancha, are a true winemaking relic of the past. Traditionally tinajas were used for fermenting out all the wine of Valdepenas, for storing wine, and in the case of the reds, for giving them some maturity. Probably one or two small, old bodegas still use them this way. However, in the best bodegas they are still used for the first part of the maturation cycle of the better red wines.

Depending on the quality of the wine, it is held in tinajas [some of which have now been replaced by concrete versions] for between six months and two years. As tinajas are earthenware, one might reasonably assume they would have some porosity, and hence that the wine could start to oxidise. This does not happen. Why it doesn't is another matter. The Valdepenans put forward various explanations: the clay is too thick, the tinaja has been fired,

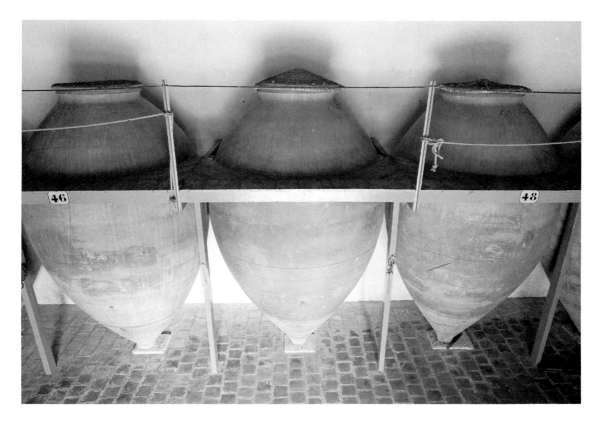

Earthenware tinajas with conical straw hats are used both to ferment and hold wine in Valdepenas.

so it takes on a kind of glaze inside, it is given a resin coating, or the tartrates thrown off by the wine form an internal, impervious coating. Nevertheless, the younger red wines *have* been in tinajas, and still keep their freshness.

Within the tinajas, the red wines throw off most of their solids, leaving a muddy sludge at the bottom of each vessel, then they are racked into clean tinajas for a further spell, or into oak casks.

The key to the development of the new Valdepenas wines is earlier picking for both red and white wines. In the case of the white wines, this, coupled with cold fermentation, gives a more fruity/floral aroma and crisper acidity. The same heightened acidity also helps the red wines last longer, but in their case it is the recent introduction of small oak barrel maturation that has done much to lift the overall quality of the better wines, the reservas and gran reservas.

New small oak barrels have uplifted the quality of many Spanish red wines, including those of Los Llanos in Valdepenas.

That there is a firm commitment to oak by the forward-thinking exporting bodegas is no better shown than at los Llanos. Here, in the middle of a rather desolate field, framed by a bank of vast stainless steel fermenters in the middle distance, is what seems to be a pretty little cantina. It hides a secret. Down a flight of whitewashed steps about nine metres underground are four vast caverns, 100 metres long, 40 metres wide, for 12,000 American oak barricas, mainly for the los Llanos red wines, but also a crianza white wine, which is unusual for the region. Such an investment in so much new oak shows the extent to which los Llanos and the other top bodegas are taking their red wines seriously.

The leading exporters of Valdepenas wine usually have two or three ranges of quality of bottled wine, with the basic range, destined for the supermarket shelves of northern Europe, comprising sound wines at inexpensive prices. However, it is their premium ranges which they hope will bring more respect for the wines of Valdepenas.

An ordinary traditional Airen white wine from Valdepenas or La Mancha is a rather plain and uninteresting beast, near characterless and with a hard edge. It is not particularly appetising. But the new Valdepenas whites, early picked and cold fermented at around 18° Centigrade, take on a different and better character. The aroma is more uplifted, with a delicate floral character. The flavour is bone dry, with a distinct salty tang in the middle, and a clean, pebbly finish. The Marques de Gastanaga of Luis Megia, the Vina Albali of Felix Solis, and the Armonioso of los Llanos are good examples. Senorio de los Llanos, the white wine that gets six months in American oak barricas, is an interesting diversion. The aroma is dry with a touch of burnt toast from the oak exposure, and the flavour firm, dry, with oaky hints. However, it is difficult to decide whether the oak has overwhelmed the wine, or enhanced its character.

Valdepenas produces some interesting commercial rosados, the best coming from lightly pressed Cencibel grapes to give the juice called *vino de yema*. They are onion-skin in colour, dry and quite firm of aroma, and bone dry, fresh, and with just enough fruit to give them personality on the palate.

The best red wines come in two distinct styles: the young, fresh and fruity ones that are successors to the traditional clarete, and which have a high proportion of Airen in their make-up, and the crianza (aged) wines. Good examples of the former are the Los Molinas 2° ano of Felix Solis, which is three parts Airen, one part Cencibel. Bright cherry red, it has a soft, fresh and fruity aroma, with a touch of almonds from the Airen, and a fresh, lightly fruity, almost sweet flavour. The very similar Marques de Gastanaga of Luis Megia is just a little drier at the finish through some time in bottle. Both epitomise the gulpable, easy drinking style of this wine. A third, more robust wine, with a pervasive blackcurrant flavour, the Bodegas Racionero Tinto, is worth mentioning because it is a rare example of an organically grown Spanish wine.

The introduction of new oak barricas to Valdepenas has encouraged the revival of mature red wines in the region. The Consejo Regulador stipulates that these wines must be at least two years in oak and bottle from the time of the harvest, though after that the choice is left to the bodegas. These wines will be made only from Cencibel, vintage dated, and while their importance to the image of Valdepenas is critical, their production is still minuscule. Only Solis, Megia, los Llanos and La Invencible have so far made the decision to invest in good wood.

Typically they will have a firm, dryish aroma with some spine from the oak, and a good, dryish and firm flavour with some fruit in the middle palate, a light tannin grip, and positive finish. Senorio de los Llanos, Luis Megia Reserva Especial and Vina Albali Reserva are the best examples.

These are not great wines by any standards, but they show what determined owners of wineries can do when they realise that their businesses and the future of their region cannot rely on supplying bread-and-butter wines alone.

Toledo

Toledo is one of the treasures of Spain. This ancient, beautiful city rises above a gorge carved by the river Tagus, and over the centuries has been turned into an artistic treasure house, quite apart from the splendour of its architecture.

It was a powerful city when Madrid was just a village, and the reminders of that power can be seen in the cathedral, with its dazzling array of paintings by Raphael, Titian, Velazquez, Rubens, Goya, Van Dyck, and above all El Greco, who spent his last years in Toledo, where his home can still be seen. The palace of El Escorial and the Alcazar vie with the cathedral for attention, and only the garish tourist shops blight this splendid city.

Cervantes wrote part of *Don Quixote* at the Posada de la Sangre, which was destroyed during the Civil War, and for centuries Toledo was the only city in western Europe where the three religions, Christian, Muslim and Jewish, lived in peace, bringing Toledo its reputation as a city of learning and intellectualism.

A little of this intellectualism rubbed off on Carlos Falco, Marques de Griñon. An agronomist by training, he went to UC Davis in California in the early 1960s to study agricultural economics. There he met the legendary viticulturalist Maynard Amerine, who showed him his research station. There, to Falco's amazement, Amerine had every vine variety grown in Spain under one roof, something Falco had not seen even in his own country. Amerine ventured the opinion that the variety best suited to many parts of Spain was Cabernet Sauvignon, and it would do well in the country around Toledo.

Falco mentally filed away this nugget of information and returned home to the 1,400 hectare estate left to him by his grandfather, in the rolling hills outside Toledo, an estate that had been in the family since the thirteenth century. His immediate concern was to begin the first commercial planting of Virginia tobacco in Spain. It was not until the early 1970s that Falco remembered Amerine's advice. He had a carrier travelling to France to collect apple trees for one of his estates, and asked the carrier also to collect some Cabernet cuttings from Bordeaux.

The carrier protested that this was illegal. 'Put them at the bottom of the pile', replied Falco. The carrier reluctantly agreed, but being a man of the Midi, he wanted to bring back Grenache instead. Falco remained adamant, and eventually received his Cabernet clones from Bordeaux.

Falco planted these cuttings on sloping land on his estate in 1973, and apart from Vega Sicilia, which had had such vines for over a century, it was one of the first plantings of this variety in Spain, and in Falco's case, unauthorised.

The estate manager wanted to uproot the vines, thinking that because the grape berries were too small they were no good, but in 1979 Falco got his first full crop of grapes.

Falco admits he had no idea what to do with the grapes. Not even Miguel Torres wanted them. After much ringing round, he eventually found a buyer in Antonio Sanz of Rueda. Sanz made his own red wine with those first grapes. A hailstorm destroyed the harvest the next year, but in 1981 Falco was back on the phone to Sanz, and eventually the two agreed to split the resulting wine and Sanz made a 50 per cent Cabernet 50 per cent Tinto Fino red wine that quickly found a buyer.

This sale spurred Carlos Falco to launch his wine under the Marques de Griñon label. By chance he met Margaux Hemingway in Madrid who led him to Alexis Lichine, owner of Chateau Priure Lichine in Bordeaux. Lichine showed the 1981 red to the great oenologist Professor Emile Peynaud, who was so interested in the potential of the wine that he has become adviser to Marques de Griñon.

Carlos Falco now has 14 hectares of Cabernet Sauvignon, and a little Merlot, planted on gently sloping land, close to the family home and chapel that were built at the time of the French Revolution. The soils are clay and calcareous stone, very similar, he says, to those of St Emilion in Bordeaux. The vineyard is at an altitude of 500 metres and gets ample sunshine, though the rainfall is low. So a trickle irrigation system has been installed, against the threat of frosts according to the owner. The vines, unusually for Spain, are high trained on the Double Guyot system, and are possibly the tallest vines anywhere in the country.

The grapes are crushed and cold fermented in stainless steel on the farm, and the wine taken to Rueda for maturation. All the wines made so far have had two years in American oak barricas before bottling, though the 1987 wine will go into one-year-old French Nevers oak. Carlos Falco realises that taking the wine all the way north to Rueda is not helping it, so he has the son of his estate manager training in cellars in Bordeaux, and will be building an underground maturation cellar on his own property in the near future.

Tasting the wines in bottle, from the 1981 blend to the 1985 Cabernet, it is clear the wines are getting better as the vines mature, and the best wines are going to come from the cooler vintages. The 1985 Cabernet is now what Marques de Griñon is all about, with a deep purple colour, an aroma showing good ripe fruit, the dusty/musty Cabernet character often found in Australian wines from this variety, a touch of beef extract, an attractive sweetness which emerges as the wine develops, and plenty of character. The flavour is full, ripe and firm, with a light oak presence, attractive fruit and good grip at the finish.

In essence it is a wine right outside the Spanish mainstream, and the introduction of French oak should give the wine more backbone and complexity.

Total annual production of the Marques de Griñon red is around 7,000 cases, and there it will stay. However, it is not an end to the winemaking ambitions of Carlos Falco. He is planning to plant Chardonnay in Rueda to give further complexity to his white Marques de Griñon which, in all honesty, it needs. And he is also looking at the Rioja, Penedes and elsewhere with a long-term view to making other high quality, limited production wines to sell under his banner.

The Toledo estate is mostly given over to the growing of barley and oats, tomatoes and sunflowers, the raising of partridges for commercial shooting, and rough land for wild boar. The vineyard only comprises a tiny 1 per cent of the estate's surface, but in many eyes it has put the name Griñon back in the public domain as one of the best of the new wave wines of Spain.

Almansa

This denominacion scarcely warrants mention except that it highlights one of the problems that the denominacion system is beginning to experience. Should an area be given denominacion of origin if so little of the wine it produces ever finishes up in bottle? Almansa is a classic case in point. It has 10,500 hectares under vine, yet only three small private producers bottle any wine at all. Nearly all Almansa wine is sold in bulk for blending. With so little wine available in bottle, and that mostly within the region of origin, it is unlikely to be found anywhere else.

Does the obscure wine from three tiny bodegas seriously warrant the importance of a denominacion? And as Almansa is not the only example—the new denominaciones of Somontano with three bottlers and Toro with two are other examples—the authorities in Madrid should think a little harder before they offer such beneficence to so few, particularly as there are many more areas in the same situation, awaiting denominacion.

It would be a great shame if Spain pursued the Italian path, with virtually every grape-growing corner of the country accorded a denominacion.

Almansa itself is a flat, featureless plain that marks the end of La Mancha and the beginning of the Levante, though clinging to La Mancha as a region. Almansa sees the end of the Airen and Cencibel and the beginning of the grape of the Levante, the red Monastrell, which, with the local grape Garnacha Tintorera and the white Merseguera, gives the three permitted varieties.

The hot continental climate, similar to that of La Mancha, produces full-bodied red wines and rosés, with alcohol levels ranging from a legal minimum of 12° up to 15°, which is why they are in demand for blending. Crianza wines must spend at least one year in wood, and be at least two years old on release.

Almansa has four basic types of wine, full-bodied rosé, full-bodied clarete, full-bodied tinto and full-bodied Garnacha Tintorera, made only from that variety. The best wines generally have the highest percentage of Monastrell.

The best wine of the region is the Vina Pandoble of Bodegas Carrion, and the other two producers who bottle wine are Bodegas Piqueras and Alfonso Abellan.

CHAPTER 8

Valencia

Valencia

Valencia is a vinous conundrum. As a region it is Spain's largest exporter of wine, accounting for some 40 per cent of total wine exports, yet its wines are relatively unknown. It is second only to La Mancha in its acreage under vine, yet within Spain is not known as a wine-producing region. Valencia produces substantial amounts of mainly red wine through its thriving wine industry, yet has only five bodegas of any importance, and three have close links to Switzerland. The city of Valencia is Spain's third largest, yet rarely do you see wine being drunk there in the bars or restaurants, and even then it is more likely to be Riojan or Catalan wine.

What lies behind Valencia's anonymity is that it has traditionally been an exporter of wine, and those exports have been in bulk, not bottle, for blending away or for bottling under a branded name for the supermarket shelves of Europe. If the wine's Valencian origins are indicated on the label, it will go largely unnoticed by the buyer. Many wine drinkers have tasted Valencia without knowing it.

The five bodegas now realise that this mask of anonymity is costing them dearly. Within Spain they are trying to attract the interest of the upmarket wine drinkers by giving their wines a chic image, while pointing out that Valencia does actually produce wine. To the average Spaniard, Valencia means oranges, rice and the home of paella and sangria. Buyers from abroad are being asked to take wine in bottle, not bulk, and preferably under the brand name of the bodega, not something a supermarket chief has dreamed up. However a glance at the labelling rooms of any bodega selling abroad, with rack upon rack of different labels for different customers, indicates that this will be a difficult battle to win.

Valencia has a long viticultural history. It was an important producing area under the Romans as its wines could be easily shipped to the tables of Imperial Rome and the colonies on the north African coast. Winemaking died away under the Arabs, but came back with the Reconquest, and as early as 1626 regulations were laid down that put Valencian wine into one of three categories: Supreme, Intermediate and Ordinary.

In the eighteenth and nineteenth centuries it was commonplace for Bordeaux shippers to strengthen their clarets with some Valencian wine, and no secret was made of it. Cyrus Redding, writing in 1833, praised the wines of the Levante, and it was not until phylloxera arrived in 1900 that the Valencian wine industry suffered any serious setback.

Though the vineyards were replanted on American rootstocks, phylloxera brought two changes to the wine industry. Before the louse arrived, most of the vineyards were planted in the rich alluvial soils of the coast. Here the growers took out their vineyards and replanted with oranges, lemons, almonds and other crops. Oranges rapidly took over as the main cash crop of Valencian agriculture, eclipsing the wine industry.

Second, the vineyards were forced into the hinterland, where the land was too poor to sustain other crops. This turned out to be a blessing in disguise as the cooler hinterland yields better quality grapes.

It is no accident that the region's wine industry is so export oriented. Valencia is Spain's first port, shipping not only a wide range of goods from other parts of Spain, but also its own produce: oranges, lemons, wine, and latterly cars, computers, shoes, toys, Lois jeans [a company founded by Valencians], carpets and textiles. As shippers and traders, the Valencians have always looked outwards.

Valencia is a very affluent part of Spain, with its wealth based both on agriculture and manufacturing. The city itself is dominated by modern apartment blocks, even in the old quarter ringed by the river Turia. The river itself has gone. When it burst its banks in 1957, drowning many citizens, General Franco built a new riverbed on the outskirts of the town, and made the old one redundant. Its 29 bridges remain, but the eight miles of the old riverbed are now being turned into the largest garden in Europe.

Everything about Valencia is brand new. Brand new concert hall, brand new offices and apartments, brand new industries. Only in the barro by the harbour can the visitor still see what old Valencia used to look like as he drives through the city en route to Benidorm.

The only real Valencian concession to the past is the curious Festival of the Fallas, held on St Joseph's day, which is also the summer solstice. Giant life-like effigies that take six months to make are displayed for three days, then, on the summer solstice, are put to the torch in a glorious, huge and unique bonfire.

The festival dates back to around 1497 when apprentice carpenters would burn their rubbish to celebrate the feast of St Joseph, their patron. Around the seventeenth century they began making small effigies called *ninots,* and from these developed the giant *fallas.* Now, every year, millions of pesetas are spent on these creations by special artists, only to go up in smoke.

Viticulturally, Valencia is quite complicated. Rising from sea level to near 800 metres, it is a web of microclimates within the province's three denominaciones of Valencia, Utiel-Requena, and Alicante to the south.

Utiel-Requena, on the central western edge of the province, is considered the best growing area, so much of its wine goes to blending wines that will be sold as Valencia. Some is bottled under the Utiel-Requena denominacion, but the two are so intermeshed that moves are afoot to incorporate them under the one denominacion Valencia. Their wines are very similar, but those of Alicante are different, so there is no suggestion that this denominacion will loose its status.

Within the denominacion Valencia there is such a difference in altitudes, climates and soils that it has been necessary to subdivide the denominacion into three, and subdivide two of those regions again.

The three sub-regions are Alto Turia, Valentino and Clariano. Alto Turia in the northern hinterland, around 625 metres above sea level, has sandy limestone soils and a semi-arid Mediterranean climate with warm summers and mild winters. It produces the best white wines of the region.

Valentino adjoins Alto Turia to the south, and is divided again into four areas: Serrania [550 metres above sea level, limestone soils, arid climate, hot dry summers, mainly white grape varieties], Campos de Liria [175 metres, limestone soils, arid climate, white wines and dessert Moscatels], Cheste [260 metres, limestone soils, arid climate, fuller white wines], and Marquesado [180 metres, limestone soils, semi-arid, mainly white wines].

Clariano is separate from the other two, to the south, at around 350 metres above sea level in undulating country with a semi-arid climate and limestone soils. It yields fuller white wines, good rosés and particularly good red wines from the Monastrell grape. It has a sub-region to the east, Valle de Albaida, with clay-limestone soils at high altitudes, around 480 metres. While much of this district is given over to table grapes, some balanced, fruity red wines are starting to come from new, higher vineyards.

With the exception of the delicate white wines of Alta Turia, these distinctions are lost to the drinker of Valencian wine, submerged in the vast blending tanks of the big bodegas. They are of interest only to the winemakers.

In total Valencia has 48,500 hectares under vine, mainly yielding white wines, while Utiel-Requena [discussed separately] has 52,700 hectares of red grape varieties, and as the exporting companies deal more in red wines and rosés than whites, it is inexorably intermeshed with Valencia as a denominacion.

Valencia also has quite a spread of permitted grape varieties compared to other denominaciones. Dry white wines and dessert wines come from the native Merseguera, Planta Fina, Pedro Ximinez, Malvasia, Moscatel and Tortosi [Bobal Blanco]. Red wines are made from Garnacha Tinta and Tintorera, Monastrell, Tempranillo and Bobal, and there are small, as yet unauthorised, but important plantings of Cabernet Sauvignon, Merlot, Cabernet Franc and Petite Syrah.

It is a varietal distinction that will once more be lost on the consumer, for again these varieties are blended, and it is unusual to come across a single varietal Valencian wine, though many rosés are made from just the Bobal grape.

Blending is the key to Valencian wine. A supermarket buyer arrives at one of the five producer bodegas, hands over the specifications of the wine he wants, the amount of acidity, alcohol and sugar, the oenologist goes away, and comes back with the model wine for the buyer, who has based his vinous prescription on customer research. It is neat, very tidy, profitable for all

In La Mancha and Valdepenas the earthenware tinajas *are still used to make red and white wines in the old way.*

The Ali Baba tinaja jars are still used to ferment wine in many Valdepenas bodegas.

La Mancha, semi-arid yet remarkably dominated by the white grape Airen.

involved, sees millions of litres of wine going abroad every year, but obscures Valencia's identity as a wine region.

It has also led these bodegas to concentrate all their efforts on producing very clean, well made fresh wines for early drinking at affordable prices. Valencian wines are not made for laying down, and while Egli for example have a crianza red wine, given a few months in new oak, at the top of their range, the amounts produced are minute in comparison to the massive 2.65 million hectolitres of wine [265 million litres] that the province [excluding Alicante] produces and sells in the course of a working year.

Because blending to a consistent style is the business of the five bodegas, there is much more similarity between their wines than is found in other parts of Spain. The typical dry Valencian white wine is fresh, crisp, exceedingly clean, with soft acidity and a light floral touch. It is based on the native Merseguera grape, usually with some Planta Fina, and often touched up with a little Moscatel. The Merseguera on its own can be a little hard and flat, but makes an ideal base wine.

The typical rosé, usually based on Bobal, and sometimes with some Garnacha, has an onion-skin colour with a touch of pink, a strong, dry aroma and flavour, plenty of body, very clean, and with a flinty dry finish. It is comparable to a Tavel rosé, but not the lighter, sweeter rosés found in many markets. In Valencia itself, these rosés, when chilled, go exceedingly well with the seafood and paella dishes native to the region, and the bodegas hope that this is the wine that will get the people of Valencia to drop their beer-drinking habits and turn to wine.

There is somewhat more variation amongst the Valencian reds, but in general they are soft, young, fruity wines, again very clean, and with a crisp acidity at the finish enhancing their freshness. As supermarket wines they are some of the best available.

Not all the wineries have embraced cold fermentation, and some of the wines show a hard, earthy edge on the palate, a one-dimensional flatness, and some of the reds a sweet, near porty middle palate, but they are in the minority.

The five important bodegas are all clustered round the harbour within walking distance of each other, in the old quarter, El Grao, of the port. The people here are fiercely independent, even from the other citizens of the city. Not so long ago the city centre and the harbour barro were quite separate areas. Now the urban sprawl has joined them physically, but not mentally, and the harbour people still consider themselves a separate breed.

The quality and consistency of Spanish wines is now constantly monitored by private and governmental laboratories.

Largest of the five bodegas is Vinival, Spain's largest wine exporting company. It was formed in 1968 by the merging of five smaller, privately-owned bodegas whose owners realised that if they were going to compete seriously in the export markets they were better off doing it together than by fighting against each other.

Three of those bodega owners, Juan Antonio Mompó, whose business was mainly with France, Erich Teschendorff, who traded mainly with Germany, and Jorge Garrigos, who concentrated on Britain, now manage Vinival, and each has sons in the business. The Steiner family, who still have a residual interest in Vinival, were one of the Swiss families in the Valencian wine trade.

The scale of Vinival is monumental. The main winery, a series of red brick, round topped cigar-shaped towers, that the locals, according to their feelings about Vinival, describe either as a cathedral or a load of suppositories, has a capacity of 33 million litres, and that capacity is turned over three times a year. Vinival annually ships around 100 million litres of wine, something like a fifth to a quarter of Spain's total wine exports.

Vinival's mode of operating is common to the other four bodegas. Must, or more commonly wine, is bought from the co-operatives of the region or other, privately-owned bodegas that do not market wine. Within the winery the blending is done in vast stainless steel, temperature-controlled tanks [other bodegas also use resin-lined cement vats], cleaned by centrifuges, the tartrates thrown off by chilling, filtered by the most modern equipment available, and bottled, again using the latest machinery, with constant laboratory supervision. These wines are as 'pure' as can be found anywhere, absolutely squeaky clean.

Vinival also has its own estate, the 160 hectare Casa de Calderon in Utiel-Requena, planted with Bobal, Garnacha and Tempranillo, and experimental plantings of Cabernet Sauvignon. This estate, and the grapes from some adjoining vineyards, form the basis for the bodega's flagship red wine, the Casa de Calderon Tinto, a soft, deep, sweet ripe fruit wine, supple and with a dry finish. The partnering white is floral and citric, fresh and with soft acids, very crisp and clean.

Vinival's second range is Torres de Serrano, named after the monument that dominates the entrance to old Valencia, and the company also produces Vival D'Oro, a lightly carbonated, sweet, grapey wine from the Moscatel grape, quite similar to an Italian *moscato,* a sweet, dessert Moscatel mistella [made by adding grape alcohol to natural, unfermented grape juice] and even a lemony wine cooler known as Breeze in Spain, Freeze elsewhere. And this is just the tip of their product range.

The Swiss-owned Bodegas Schenk is a winery with the unusual distinction of also being the Swiss consulate in Valencia. Founded in 1927, it too brings in wine from the co-operatives, or must to vinify itself for its higher quality wines. Schenk has a turnover of between 35,000 and 50,000 hectolitres a year, with its main wines the Castillo Murviedro and Cavas Murviedro reds, whites and rosés, and the premium Real Copero moscatel and San Terra wood-aged [in Limousin oak] red, both coming in unusual handmade bottles. The San Terra, made only from Monastrell grapes, is deep, dry and pungent, with a slightly toasted aroma, but much smoother and suppler than the aroma suggests, with some interesting Burgundian overtones.

Bodegas Augusto Egli and Vicente Gandia Pla are across the street from each other. Egli was founded in 1903 by a Zurich wine merchant, and remains Swiss owned. At the time of the Civil War the French traders, who also had a strong interest in Valencia, all left, but the Swiss remained.

With a capacity of 8 million litres, Egli is another monument to stainless steel, modern bottling lines and quality control.

Egli has owned the Casa Lo Alto estate in Utiel-Requena since the beginning of the decade, and here it is experimenting with the likes of Cabernet Sauvignon, Cabernet Franc and Petite Syrah, but at the moment no decision has been made on what will happen to the wine made from these varieties. The flagship Casa Lo Alto Tinto is currently made from Tempranillo and Garnacha, and displays a big, perfumed, sweet aroma, plump, soft flavour, and a firm dry finish. The wine is given extra character after 3 to 6 months in new American oak, and with the San Terra of Schenk shows there is a future for crianza reds in Valencia.

The Casa Lo Alto white is equally unusual in that it is made from Macabeo, one of the varieties of Penedes, and shows the soft, floral fruitiness and freshness that this variety gives when cold fermented. At Egli they think Macabeo is one of the most promising white grapes for the region.

Other Egli wines come under the Rey Don Jaime and Perla Valencia names, and the Rey Don Jaime Blanco is one of the few examples of a wholly Merseguera wine, and also one from Alto Turia. It gives an interesting liquorice touch to the aroma, and attractive tangy finish to the palate.

Of the wine shipped from Valencia, 85 per cent is in bulk, the balance in bottle. Vicente Gandia Pla are the largest exporters in bottle with their very typical Castillo de Liria and the new Floreal wines. The Castillo de Liria Tinto typifies Valencian red wines with its bouncy young fresh fruit aroma, and young, soft, fresh flavour with a crisp finish. A very gulpable wine that would even take to a light chill in the summer in the manner of beaujolais nouveau.

Founded in 1885 by Vicente Gandia, and now owned and run by his grandson José Maria, the company typifies the Valencian belief in its wineries through the recent building of a superb new facility at Chiva, outside the city, with a capacity of 250,000 hectolitres, and fermentation tanks that can deal with up to 100,000 litres of wine each.

Another monument to stainless steel and temperature control, this new winery could be airlifted to California's Napa Valley and be completely at home. Within Spain, it is hi-tech to the extreme.

The fifth main winery is the smallest and most traditional, but it is still a large winery by Spanish standards. The charmingly named Cherubino Valsangiacomo of Swiss birth founded his winery in 1900, and it is still owned by the family. In the old timber roofed winery some fermentation is still done in the big, open oak *cubas* [vats] and the Vall de Sant Jaume white does show a slight hardness. However the Vall de Sant Jaume 1975 red shows just how well Valencian reds, even without the help of oak, will hold on to life. Dry, slightly earthy, and with a meat extract touch on the nose, and a supple, dryish flavour, with a hint of sweetness, light bodied and very accessible, it was still very much there after a dozen years.

In an ideal world, the Valencian bodegas would like appropriate recognition for the wines they are producing. They know they are not going to be the Rioja of the south, but nor do they expect to be. However with their scrupulously clean and well made day-to-day wines they are satisfying many wine drinkers, and feel it would be proper for those people to know what wine they are drinking.

Their aim is to sell more wine in bottle, and to lift quality. Valencia produces oranges, wine and computers, just like California, said one member of the industry. It is a point worth remembering.

Utiel–Requena

Though a denominacion in its own right, Utiel-Requena is tightly bound to its neighbouring denominacion Valencia. Formed through the combining of two smaller denominacions, there is now debate on whether Utiel-Requena should itself be merged with Valencia. While this suggestion has not met with wholehearted approval in Utiel, it does have merit.

Valencia is more a white wine denominacion, while Utiel is predominantly red and rosé country. More importantly, the bulk of its wine production goes to blending and eventual sale not with the name Utiel on the label, but Valencia, so in a de facto way a merger has already taken place in part.

For the time being, Utiel is vitally important to the big Valencian bodegas as the source of the millions of litres of red and rosé wines they export. Utiel is recognised as the best part of the province for growing red wine grapes, and unlike Valencia, its vineyard area is increasing. With 52,700 hectares planted, it is already larger than Valencia [with 48,500 hectares under vine], and yields 1.35 million hectolitres.

It is the highest part of the province, on its western edge bordering on the great Central Plateau of Spain. Vineyards are planted up to 725 metres above sea level, yet despite this altitude the climate is semi-arid and rather extreme, with summer temperatures reaching 40° Centigrade, and winters as cold as minus 5° Centigrade. These conditions call for tough grape varieties, and in the Bobal, with its small tight bunches of black grapes, the region has one. However, the Bobal does not give great red wines on its own, so Tempranillo in particular, and also Garnacha, are being recommended for new plantings.

Utiel's red wines are generally a blend of two or all three of these varieties, though the best wines are now Tempranillo with some Garnacha, and if the wine goes to Valencia for blending the Monastrell variety also comes into the picture.

Bobal is also used extensively to make the rosé wines of the region, and, as a by-product, *doble pasta*. First, the free-run juice of the Bobal is taken off after light skin contract, and vinified into rosé. To the roughly 30 per cent of the mass of the grapes left, more bunches are added and the mass is vinified to give a deep, strong wine that is ideal for blending as the doble pasta.

As in Valencia, the lion's share of the vinification of wines in Utiel is done by large co-operatives, who then sell the wine on to the big Valencian bodegas to polish up, bottle and merchandise to the big wine buyers. Very little is bottled for selling with the Utiel denominacion indicated on the label. However, these soft, ripe and fruity wines are high quality when it comes to inexpensive, daily drinking wines.

Las Falleras Tinto from Bodegas Schenk, a blend of Tempranillo and Garnacha [Cencibel], has a hint of violets on the nose, and a soft, savoury flavour, a touch grippy at the finish, and is one example of a Utiel wine in bottle.

Vincente Egli have their Casa Lo Alto estate in this region, where they have planted imported varieties like Cabernet Sauvignon and Cabernet Franc, and use American oak over a short period to their current Utiel red wine, also Tempranillo and Garnacha.

They bottle three wines with the denominacion Utiel-Requena. The soft, fresh, lightly flowery Casa Lo Alto Blanco is made from Macabeo, a variety that is slowly being introduced to the province. The Rey Don Jaime Baco de Oro has the deep, dry, though quite supple and fresh style of the rosé wines of Valencia. As the province has hot weather for most of the year, these rosés are perfect alternatives to the red wines.

The Casa do Alto Tinto shows the plump ripe fruit aroma and flavour, the softness in the middle palate, and the firmness at the finish that the best Valencian reds have.

Egli also play around with three other Utiel red wines. Rey Don Jaime Tinto has a soft, smooth flavour, nicely balanced, while the Rey Don Jaime Reserva gets some oak exposure, and hence has a spicier, firmer nature. The most unusual wine of the three is Diego Montosa, which has some residual sugar in it, giving a very soft, fruity character with a delicate sweetness to the finish.

The Casa Calderon wines of Vinival, named after their large Utiel estate, are not necessarily Utiel wines, as the estate name is used as a brand. However, the Casa Calderon Tinto, a soft, deep, supple wine with plenty of dry extract, blended from Garnacha, Bobal and Monastrell, has its origins in the denominacion.

Experiments with the two Cabernets and Merlot by Vicente Egli and Vinival in the Utiel region may reveal a whole new future for Utiel-Requena. However if the takeover bid by Valencia goes through, it will be Valencia that ultimately gets the reward as one of Spain's least-known denominaciones simply fades away.

CHAPTER 9

Murcia

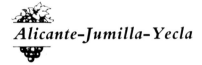

Alicante-Jumilla-Yecla

The three denominaciones of origin Alicante, Jumilla and Yecla sit side by side, and in terms of wine styles there is not much to separate one from another. They are part of the south-east of Spain traditionally known as the Levante.

It is an historic part of Spain that remained largely undeveloped and undiscovered until the recent advent of tourism. Now the pretty seaside fishing village of Benidorm has become one of the best-known destinations for tourists seeking the warmth of the Spanish sun. Just to the north of Alicante itself, Benidorm is the jewel of the Costa Blanca, and now a permanent home for many expatriates attracted to the region by its sandy beaches, warm and healthy climate, and the string of picturesque villages along the coast.

Palm trees, olives, and thousands of orange and almond trees thrive in the fertile coastal soils, as this is the beginning of the Garden of Spain, stretching down along the coast south from Alicante. Just 14 miles from that town is Elche, the melon capital, also renowned for the palm trees that traditionally supplied the long fronds that throughout the region were carried to Mass on the Sunday before Easter. It was also the site of the discovery of the famous Lady of Elche, a statue thought to be of Celtic origin and over 3,000 years old. It is now a national treasure.

The holiday villas, sandy beaches, market gardens, fishing villages and clear waters of the coast are a vivid contrast to the hard, unchanging life of the farmers just a few miles inland. The hilly hinterland, the north-eastern extremity of the Sierra Nevadas, is semi-arid, with baking summers and very little rain throughout the year. A downpour often means flash flooding, and the farmers have to struggle to raise their crops, largely unable to rely on one product for their livelihood. It is an agricultural backwater of Spain.

It has long been an area where vines are grown, and in the middle of the last century was known for a red dessert wine called Fondillon, which survives today, but only in tiny quantities. When the phylloxera louse began devastating the northern vineyards, the vineyards of Alicante, Yecla and Jumilla had their golden age. Around the turn of the century the area planted expanded rapidly, but the louse found its way to Alicante and Yecla, sparing only Jumilla because of its sandy soils, and the region sank back into relative obscurity.

Recently the international demand for sound, inexpensive wines has brought a measure of prosperity back to the region, but it remains a source of blending and bulk wine, and in terms of quality and the development of new wines, it remains very much a lower middle-class area.

Across the region the soils are predominantly limestone, with Jumilla having deep, sandy soils as well. The climate is Mediterranean, with long, hot summers, but coupled with the lack of rain it means a region better suited to the production of deep red wines than delicate whites, and red wine accounts for nearly all its production.

The drought-resistant Monastrell red grape of the Penedes dominates plantings, though Garnacha Tintorea, Cencibel [the Tempranillo of the Rioja] and the Bobal of Valencia are also permitted. White wines are primarily made from the Airen of La Mancha, another drought-resistant variety, the local Verdil, and the Valencian Merseguera. Because of the climate they are trained as low bush vines to catch any early morning dew, retain moisture in the soil, and protect the bunches from the fierce summer sun which the Benidorm tourists love, but the vine growers don't.

Production throughout the region is dominated by co-operatives that vinify the grapes and either sell the wine in bulk or to bodegas who mature and bottle under their own names. The exception is the La Purisma co-operative of Yecla, which bottles and sells in its own right.

The denominacion Alicante in the Province of Valencia, with a spur into Murcia, is the coastal region of the three. Its 27,000 hectares are spread inland in the mountain valleys, and the lower slopes. Though a little white wine is made, and the higher, cooler mountain slopes could, in theory, yield lighter, fresher whites, it is red wine country and the Monastrell is king.

The only wines that can carry the denominacion are the reds, rosés and doble pasta. The latter is a by-product of making rosés. The *vino de lagrima* [free run] juice is run off the crushed grapes, giving very little skin contact, then the remaining slush is pressed to give doble pasta. It really is not a wine for drinking, but can be used in a blend. In his book *The Wines of Spain,* Jan Read quotes one local winemaker as saying of doble pasta: 'If it gets onto your suit, don't bother to have it cleaned. Cut the patch out.'

A dozen co-operatives account for almost all the Alicante wine made, but they sell on to private bodegas who merchandise it, or supply in bulk. Some reserva and gran reserva wines are worth looking for, particularly the Costa Blanca of Garcia Poveda. His namesake, Salvador Poveda, is one of the few to carry on the old tradition of making a Fondillon wine from Monastrell grapes, a *generoso* wine as they call it in Spain, which has a vague affinity with port. But generally the best wines of Alicante are the fresh but generous rosés that encourage the afternoon siesta on the Costa Blanca.

Yecla is the smallest of the three denominaciones, sandwiched between the other two. It is the northern tip of Murcia, again hilly and semi-arid, and again dominated by red wine production, though once more its best wines are the rosés, which have an affinity with those of Tavel in France.

Production is dominated by the vast Cooperativa La Purisma, with its capacity running to 55 million litres of wine. It markets a range of its own wines under the Yecla and Calp names, which have had some success internationally, but at best are honest, day-to-day wines. The private bodega of Enrique Ochoa Palao has a local following for its red and rosé wines.

Jumilla, the furthest inland, with the town of the same name 100 kilometres from Alicante, lies mostly in the province of Albacete, the rest in Murcia. In the hilly to mountainous terrain, with steep-sided, rugged river valleys, local farmers toil for their crops. The land is mostly only suitable for vines, olive and almond trees, and grapes are the mainstay of the local economy.

The grape growers are fortunate to have in their midst the Cooperativa San Isidro, rivalling La Purisma in size, and generally considered to be one of the most efficient, thoroughly modern co-operatives in Spain. Again the emphasis at San Isidro is on red and rosé wines, and the co-operative has become a mecca for foreign buyers looking for such wines in bulk. This explains the rapid expansion of the Jumilla vineyards at a time when many other areas are static or contracting. Jumilla is also helped by having sandy, phylloxera-free soils, so it is one of the few parts of Spain where the expensive grafting of the vines onto louse-resistant American rootstocks does not have to be done.

San Isidro bottles a little wine under the Sabatacha, Rumor, Zambra and Solera names for export. Tiny amounts of wine from private local bodegas including Bleda, Senorio del Condestable, Juvinsa, José Menor Fernadez, Carrion, Rosendo and Asensio Carcelen trickle onto foreign tables, but it is in the Costa Blanca bars that they are most likely to be found.

Since the turn of the century there has been a strongish French influence on winemaking in Alicante, Yecla and Jumilla, but to date not even French expertise can conquer the Levantine climate, and it remains a source of decent if unexciting wines for dinner tables from Manchester to Moscow.

CHAPTER 10

Andalucia

Jerez–Sherry

Sherry is Spain's best-known drink, the one it has been shipping abroad for centuries to grace the taverns and tables of the world. Shakespeare knew of it as sack, a deep amber wine, and made Falstaff in Henry IV its devoted admirer. 'Give me a cup of Sack: I am a rogue, if I drunk today', he exclaims.

Until recently, sherry was the one international drink to come from Spain, the one most wine drinkers would have heard of, if not enjoyed. Now, with the renaissance of the table wine industry, other names like Rioja and Penedes are competing for attention and sherry, for once, has had to share the Spanish stage.

Sherry comes from the triangle of land between Jerez, Puerto de Santa Maria and Sanlucar de Barrameda in southern Andalucia, between Seville and Cadiz. The casual visitor to the home of the sherry dynasties would be impressed by the old world charm, the leisured manner, the quiet civility of the sherry families, the timelessness of the sherry business. The visitor could be forgiven for thinking that nothing much changes from year to year. The visitor would be wrong. In both vineyard techniques and in making wine, the sherry people are as advanced as anywhere in

Spain, and have contributed much to the development of the industry. And as a group they have just gone through a major upheaval in the structure of the industry which has seen them emerge as a more tight-knit body than ever in the past, facing the future with confidence.

In making their wine, the Jerezanos have long had to live with one of the most complicated, lengthy and near mysterious processes in the wine world. The key to sherry, the unique interaction between the new wine and a special yeast known as flor, is why sherry has such a special taste, and what makes it one of the world's finest aperitifs.

Other countries also produce sherry style wines, just as other countries make wines in the manner of champagne. But none captures that special taste, and with sherry it is due to the flor. A story has it that an Australian winemaker, frustrated in his attempts to make a sherry, came to Jerez and while touring a cellar was able to filch a test tube of flor from the surface of a cask. He returned home and the flor did make a wine like sherry, but it would never be quite the same.

Flor is the key to sherry, but other elements make their contribution: the soil, the climate, characterised by the luminescent, almost blinding skies of the area—the same skies that travellers to Greece marvel at—the proximity of the sea, the way the wine is made, and the unique way in which it changes to sherry and is matured.

Nature has pretty much defined where the sherry grapes are grown within the triangle. In the past this was a littoral deposit that time sculpted into a series of low, curvaceous hills and valleys. The hills are composed of chalky soils, known as *albariza*, blindingly white in the summer as the sun hits them, and in stark contrast to the green of the neat rows of vines.

In the valleys is a much heavier, deep grey clay soil known as *barro*, and there are outcrops of a light sandy soil called *arena*. Time has shown that these latter soils produce a much coarser sherry, so they have been given over to other crops like cereals, sunflowers for oil, and tobacco. The albariza has been reserved for the vines.

In the past a multiplicity of varieties were used to make sherry, but again time has whittled them down to just two, the Palomino, and the Pedro Ximinez, which is grown in small quantities to make a specific style of sherry. The Palomino, which dominates plantings, has two branches of the family. The Palomino de Jerez held sway for many years, but the Palomino Fino, a subtly different version that was located near Sanlucar, is now used for most new plantings. All three are white grapes, small, and not very pleasant to eat.

The application of science to viticulture is nowhere more evident in Spain than in these vineyards, for no other reason than that the Jerezanos are basically dealing with only one grape variety, so they need to get the best out of it. In recent years there has been much research done into the more obscure aspects of viticulture like clonal selection, the process of selecting the healthiest plants from which cuttings will be taken to propagate into new vines, the control of vineyard pests and viruses, and the best way to train vines that will have to face a searingly hot summer every year of their life. The results of this research, this fine tuning, has spread not only to other parts of Spain, but around the world.

The lack of rainfall, and the decision of the Jerezanos not to irrigate, means the vines have to struggle during the summer months, sending their roots very deep to find water. Often the area is gripped by drought, the vines look listless, and when the picking starts in September the grapes are small and hard. Yet, say the Jerezanos, these battling grapes give the best juice.

The hardened vineyard workers and their families, often labouring in temperatures that would drive most people indoors, pick the grapes delicately into containers developed in Jerez that catch every drop of juice from any broken grapes and do not let those on top crush those at the bottom by sheer weight. They are trucked to the waiting wineries as quickly as possible.

Not so long ago these grapes would have been crushed by men wearing *zapatos*, special shoes with nail studded soles. Now it is a colourful reminder of the past sometimes displayed for the benefit of special visitors. Instead the grapes go to modern presses for, as with every other aspect of winemaking, Jerez is as modern as anywhere.

Much research has been done into this part of the cycle, for the Jerezanos have found that the harder the grapes are pressed, the less delicate the resulting sherries will be, and the trend now is to use gentle pneumatic presses.

The new juice, the *mosto*, is run off into tanks where it is allowed to settle and throw off some of its solids, then the fermentation that will turn it into wine begins. Strains of wild yeast exist naturally in the vineyards, and some producers let these yeasts start the fermentation. However, the major cellars now use cultivated yeasts, developed in their laboratories, killing the wild yeasts off first with chemicals, then inoculating the wine with the house-trained yeasts. Again this is an area of intense research: the Jerezanos have a vested interest in understanding as much as they can about yeasts.

The new wine is a light white wine, not particularly high in alcohol, with the more delicate ones considered the best. Variations exist largely due to the location of the vineyards, with some areas giving very delicate wines, others more full bodied.

The new wine is then run off into casks called *butts,* and taken to the cellars or bodegas of the sherry houses. Here the second fermentation takes place and the famous flor, literally meaning flower, begins to grow on the wine.

The Jerezanos admit that they still do not fully understand the intricacies of the interaction between flor and wine. It is an act of nature. Experience has taught them that to some extent they can manipulate and predict what the flor will provide, but they can never be totally certain what the flor will produce from butt to butt.

The butts are never fully filled, for the flor needs space to grow. The other unusual aspect is that the cellarmasters also want the air to interact with the wine, to oxidise it partially—something most other winemakers try strenuously to avoid.

The flor grows like a thin white carpet on the surface of the wine, growing spontaneously, feeding off the remaining sugar in the wine, and through a more complex chemical interaction it develops the unique sherry flavour. On a more prosaic note it perfumes the air of the sherry towns at the height of the cycle with a strange but not unpleasant scent.

Gradually the flor finds no more sustenance in the wine and begins to die, the dead cells falling to the bottom of the cask. It is possible to keep a flor going by adding new wine, but most houses are content to let the cycle run its course.

In the spring after the vintage the first classification is made of the wine, and the best casks are marked as such by the *capataz,* the highly skilled head of the bodega with years of experience. Basically there are two types of sherry, fino and oloroso, and it is the flor that decides. In years to come, man may be able to make the decision by controlling the flor, but at the moment the yeast makes up its own mind.

Those casks where the flor has grown vigorously will become finos, and if necessary are sparingly fortified with alcohol to around 15 degrees, and left for a longer period on the yeasts. Those where the flor has been less effective in its efforts will be earmarked as olorosos and fortified to 18 degrees, killing any

The venenciador, using a special cup on a rod, can draw a cask sample and pour it from above his head without spilling a drop.

remaining active yeasts. A third and rare category is the palo cortado, a wine uncertain as to whether it is a fino or oloroso style; in some cases, when the flor has not taken properly, it leaves a coarser wine known as a raya.

It is now known as *anada* wine, or wine of the year. The oloroso clear wine is taken off the dead yeasts, the fino style left longer to develop the flavour.

Within this rather elementary classification is a multiplicity of options, again determined by the capataz. Day after day he tastes from cask to cask, plunging his *venencia*—with a spiral hook on one end, a small cup on the other, and a flexible whalebone of cane stem in between—into the wine. He draws his sample, whisks the venencia above his head, and from a metre or so pours an accurate

Garnacha, the red grape of Valencia.

Mesas carved by erosion break the featureless plain of La Mancha. In Valencia bush vines are the standard.

stream of wine into the small copita, the special glass of Jerez. It looks simple, but those visitors who try it invariably pour the wine down the front of their clothes.

A very delicate fino will be sent to Sanlucar on the coast where it will develop into the driest of all sherries, the manzanilla, with a salty tang said to come from the sea breezes that blow through the bodegas. Slightly fuller finos will be matured in Jerez or Puerto. Those with the greatest vinosity will be earmarked as amontillados. The rare palo cortados will be left to their own devices, while the best olorosos will be earmarked as such, and those not quite so fine will become the cream and pale cream sherries.

The next stage of the cycle is also virtually unique to Jerez: the maturation of the wine. No two casks of new sherry are the same, but it would be unacceptable to both the producers and the consumers if each bottle tasted slightly different. So the Jerezanos have developed what is both a blending and maturation system known as the solera system.

In their bodegas, always above ground to allow the air to circulate, they practise what can be described as a fractional blending system. Once the flor has done its work, and the capataz has decided what the flor has done, the anada wine goes to a criadera or nursery. In the bodegas are row upon row of butts stacked four, five or six high. The mother is the solera, and she will be supported by five or six criaderas.

The anada wine goes into the first year criadera from which a smallish proportion of wine is taken to pass on to the second criadera, and in turn some of that wine passes to the third, fourth and fifth criaderas, and eventually to the solera itself, where the percentage of wine drawn off to make way for wine from the oldest criadera goes to the bottling lines.

At each stage the younger wine takes on the characteristic of the older wine it is joining. Some of the soleras in use were laid down with their supporting criaderas back in the last century, and a mature sherry drawn from the solera can have a minute quantity of wine going back 100 years or more in its composition.

The length of time allocated for the wine to pass through the solera system really depends on the style of sherry. About nine months is a minimum time, but in practice the best of the younger, fresher manzanillas and finos would get longer, amontillados a matter of years running into decades for the finest wines, and olorosos much the same.

The soleras are the blending and maturation arms of each sherry house, and though a slight adjustment may be made to the final wine before bottling, particularly in terms of colour or sweetness, what comes out of the solera is pretty much the finished sherry . So little wonder that the soleras it has laid down are the most valuable asset of each sherry house.

This rather lengthy description of how sherry is made also highlights an important aspect of sherry. With the exception of the fine old tawny ports of Portugal, I cannot think of any other wine region where so much wine is tied up for such a lengthy period of time. Even the greatest chateaux of Bordeaux only hold their wine for the length of the maturation cycle, about two years. So it is remarkable, if you compare the price of sherry to other fine wines, just how inexpensive it is.

Equally, sherry is a versatile drink, with a range of flavours to suit different occasions. The driest, lightest and freshest style is the manzanilla of Sanlucar, with its distinctive salty tang. Curiously, if you move a manzanilla from Sanlucar to bodegas in Jerez, it takes on the deeper characteristic of a fino, but a fino can never be converted to a manzanilla by travelling in the opposite direction.

Fino, the staple diet of the sherry trade, the style that sells all over the world and on which the reputation and livelihood of most sherry houses is based, is a little fuller, a shade stronger, a touch more vinous than a manzanilla, but is still a fresh, crisp and dry wine. Both should always be served chilled, and drunk either as an aperitif or with fish and white meat dishes.

Indeed, in the sherry triangle you rarely see them drinking anything else during lunch or dinner, particularly with the stunning array of fish and shellfish dishes plucked fresh from the nearby sea, including, around ten different varieties of prawns.

However, it is not quite as dangerous as it sounds, because the manzanillas and finos of Jerez are lighter in alcohol than those shipped for export, where a little more fortification is needed to help them survive the journey. In fact they are about the same strength as some of the bigger Californian Chardonnays, of which I remember one that would have made an average fino taste thin and weedy.

If a fuller fino is either fortified a little more and left to pass through the solera at a slower pace, or left on its own, it ages into an amontillado, amber coloured with a distinctive nutty aroma, deeper flavour, yet bone dry. Very old ones are mouth puckering with their dry, intense flavour.

An amontillado can be treated as an aperitif, a mid afternoon drink, or can be served with fuller dishes and roasts.

Palo cortado, the undecided sherry, is rare. It has something of the style of an amontillado, and something of an oloroso, very full bodied and intense in flavour, pungent and powerful.

If fino is the right arm of the sherry trade, oloroso is the left. It is a full, deep, perfumed sherry, nutty, golden brown, quite strong, and with a soft but quite dry flavour when it is true to character, and can live to a venerable age. In recent years there has been some bastardisation of the style through the use of sweetening agents to give a more popular style, but a genuine oloroso is a fine wine indeed, and best served at the end of a meal with something like a bowl of nuts.

Oloroso is also the palette on which the now popular sweet sherries are made. Here is where the other grape of Jerez, the Pedro Ximinez, comes in. Traditionally the whole bunches of grapes are picked and laid on straw mats exposed to the Andalucian sun, where they shrivel, desiccate and become raisins with a concentrated flavour. When vinified they produce a thick, almost syrupy wine that tastes like a bite into a handful of raisins, sweet and sugary.

When a little is added to an old oloroso it produces an amoroso, a quite rare sherry with a rich but smooth flavour, heady perfume, but the best finishing quite dry. However the major style based on oloroso and Pedro Ximinez is the British invention, the cream sherry, first and still typified today by Harvey's Bristol Cream. A deep nut brown colour, fruity sweet on the nose, full and sweetish on the palate, it is a popular, anytime sherry, though not very well suited to food.

The distaff side is the pale cream sherry, as personified by Croft Original, and a relative newcomer. It is made by adding to a fino what is known as dulce apagado, a wine where the fermentation has been stopped by the addition of brandy, leaving residual sugar. They are a creamy yellow colour with a full, sweetish aroma and flavour, but the finest, and they can be fine, have an unusual flor, almost yeasty scent, and clean, fresh finish.

There are some rarely seen sherries too. Brown sherry, as personified by Don Zoilo, is a deep, almost opaque brown, with a rich aroma and deep, full-bodied, sweet flavour. Pedro Ximinez, again personified by Don Zoilo, is almost treacly thick and very sweet, but pour some over ice cream and it is delicious. Old landed sherries, amontillados, palo cortados and olorosos, are wines that have been shipped by traditional British wine merchants, like Harvey's of Bristol, in cask, and are held in their cellars while they deepen in intensity, and become drier over the years.

Emilio Lustau have developed a range of almacanista sherries, in tiny quantities. An almacanista is a dying breed in Jerez, a connoisseur who buys his or her own sherries in cask and lays them down, usually for their own personal enjoyment. They are usually single vineyard, single-cask sherries of finesse, and will name the owner and the vineyard. Lustau have also resurrected Old East India, a deep, rich oloroso style, and Vino de Pasto, a light bodied oloroso with a nod towards a full fino, both sherries once shipped by British merchants, and both for drinking after dinner.

All the important sherry houses, no matter where they are based, offer a complete range of the main styles, and many have a superior range to complement their day-to-day range.

The sherry capital is, without question, Jerez. Its full name is Jerez de la Frontera, a gracious title awarded in recognition of the town's long time role as a frontline buttress of the Spanish Catholics in their great struggle to rid their country of the Moors. The Moors ruled Jerez for more than five centuries, from 711 to around 1260 AD, successors to Phoenicians, Greeks, Romans and Goths. They left their imprint on Jerez in the plazas with their tinkling fountains and shady palm trees, the orange trees that line the streets of the old town, the tiled mosaics and floors of the grander buildings. With reconquest by the armies of Castille, the Spanish influence was imposed, and part of the strong fortified walls built to resist the still threatening Moors survive today.

The old part of Jerez retains its charm, with a tangle of cobbled streets, whitewashed buildings, tiny bars, the courtyarded homes of the grander families, an old world charm reflected in its people and the languid air that belies a town built on international commerce.

Hidden behind long, whitewashed walls, each bearing the proud name of its owner, are the vaulted bodegas of the great sherry houses, high roofed, cool and classical buildings where row upon row of butts hold the maturing sherry. Here the visitor will find the headquarters of Domecq, Gonzalez Byass, Garvey, Sandeman, John Harvey, Emilio Lustau—whose bodega incorporates a vaulted dome, thought to be the guard room of the Moorish garrison—Palomino & Vergara, Sanchez Romate, De Soto, La Riva, Wisdom & Warter, Williams & Humbert and the like.

The strong British influence on the development of the sherry trade can be seen in many of these and other names: Croft; Sandeman; John William Burdon; the Byass half of Gonzalez Byass; Garvey; John Harvey, who shipped sherries from their inception in 1796, only bought their first bodega in 1970, but are

Cool vaulted Garvey bodegas where the new wine goes through a complicated process over many years to emerge as sherry.

now a major presence in Jerez; Osborne; even the formidable and Spanish-sounding Domecq, founded by the Irishman Patrick Murphy: all trace their origins back to the British Isles.

Over the years there has been much intermarriage between the British and the Spanish Jerezanos, and the scions of the big sherry houses often seem more British than the British themselves. There has also been much intermarriage between the sherry families themselves, and it is not unusual to be welcomed to a Gonzalez bodega by a Domecq, or to a Domecq bodega by a Gonzalez.

121

The sherry boom of the early 1970s, which allowed the rise of the Rumasa empire of the Zoilo Ruiz Mateos family, nearly broke these centuries-old ties. Rumasa gobbled up bodega after bodega on an unprecedented scale. There was a wall on one of the arterial roads of Jerez where Rumasa listed the bodegas it owned. The other sherry shippers used to drive by, wondering who would be next. They called it 'The wall of death'.

Rumasa's aggressive policy of undercutting the other houses to build a market share and generate cash to finance further acquisitions, swamped the market with cheap sherry and brought the industry to its knees. Only the government sequestration of the Rumasa empire and its break-up, plus a new concerted and mutually agreed policy by the other major sherry producers, brought them back from the brink to a new period of relative prosperity. Most weathered the storm not through their sherry sales but through their parallel production of Spanish brandy.

It is not widely discussed in the context of Jerez and the sherry industry, but the sherry houses dominate the production of brandy within Spain. The country is a huge consumer of brandy, around ten million cases a year, which is the equivalent of four bottles per head, man, woman and child.

It was these sales that helped keep the bodegas afloat, though no one would have foreseen it during the boom of the early 1970s. That boom, and the pressure it put on maturation space in the old town, saw the rise of new bodegas on its outskirts, notably the hugely expensive Bodegas Internacionales, headquarters of the burgeoning Rumasa empire, the adjoining Las Copas bodega of Gonzalez Byass, the Bobadillo bodega, and the new Rancho Croft. They now jostle with the ugly highrise apartment blocks that ring old Jerez, a blight to be found in all the Mediterranean countries.

On the road to Cadiz is the old port of Puerto de Santa Maria, from where much of the sherry was once shipped and a little still is. Now Puerto de Santa Maria tends more to rely on its fishing fleet for traffic. It is virtually unspoilt and renowned for its tapas bars where the locals enjoy their sherry with seemingly endless little dishes of tapas, or nibbles, that can be anything from a slice of cold paella or cured ham, nuts, olives, spicy sausage, tiny fried fish, squid, shrimp, a dozen kinds of prawns, whelks or mussels.

Puerto is home to several famous bodegas in Osborne and its affiliate Duff Gordon, the united banners of Luis Caballero, La Cuesta and John William Burdon, and Fernando de Terry, recently purchased by Harvey's, who also inherited the beautiful stable of the rare white Andalucian Cartujanos horses, housed in the old bodegas of Burdon.

The third town of the sherry triangle is Sanlucar de Barrameda, on the coast. Home of manzanilla sherry and a string of fine seafood restaurants supplied by its fishing fleet, sleepy Sanlucar will, in 1992, be the scene for a massive celebration to mark the 500th anniversary of the discovery of America, for it was from here that Christopher Colombus set sail to find the New World.

Sanlucar has a dozen and a half bodegas, but as far as sherry goes it is dominated by Antonio Barbadillo, whose sprawling bodegas, around their charming, courtyarded offices, are almost a town within a town. Quite apart from a joint venture with Harvey's, they supply much of the manzanilla bottled by other sherry houses, while also shipping in their own right. Smaller bodegas with some international sales include Delgado Zuleta, Hidalgo, Pedro Romero, José Medina, Perez Marin, Manuel Baron, Cayd, Antonio Parra Guerrero, Argueso, Otaolaurruchi and the charmingly named Los Infantes Orleans-Bourbon. I wonder whose wines Colombus took with him.

A week in Jerez can leave the visitor with a craving for a decent glass of red or white wine, for the Jerezanos drink little else but sherry with food. So far only Antonio Barbadillo with their Castillo de San Diego dry white wine, made by cold fermentation techniques, have done anything about using the Palomino grape to make anything but sherry, though de Terry is on the verge of releasing a table wine. I have also heard that a pied noir from Algeria has been planting Cabernet Sauvignon grapes in the area, but so far I have not encountered the wine, though a few Jerezanos who have tasted it say it is not bad. Another toe in a different stream is the rich dessert wine made by Paez Morrila in Arcos de la Frontera, described as a Spanish Muscat Beaumes de Venise.

Apart from their women, the Jerezanos have three other loves besides sherry and fine food—bull-fighting, horses and flamenco dancing. The area around Jerez has long been famous for breeding some of Spain's best fighting bulls, and at the Plaza de Toros in Jerez a corrida is as authentically Spanish as anything to be found in Spain.

William Garvey, founder of the eponymous sherry house, is credited with the introduction of horse-breeding in the region, and the Andalucian School of Equestrian Art in Jerez holds a display every Thursday, which can put its Viennese rival to shame.

It supplies many of the dancing horses for Vienna. The locals love every aspect of equestrianism, including polo, and celebrate the horse with their annual parade through Jerez in mid-May.

Flamenco dancing is at its best during the Vendimia festival to celebrate the grape harvest, held in early September. Young women carry the first grapes up the steps of the Collegiate church, where they are blessed and then carried to waiting vineyard workers who crush them with their feet, and as the first juice flows the church bells start ringing, a massive shout comes from the audience, pigeons are released and a week of celebration begins, with a parade through the streets and celebrating into the dawn in the park of Jerez. A reactionary mayor who thought this was too rich for the blood of the citizens of Jerez recently put a block on the nightly festivities in the park. But he has recanted, and once again some of the finest flamenco dancers in Spain come to Jerez each year to show their skills.

It is an entirely Andalucian celebration, one that is spontaneous, and while the visitor is welcome it is a festival that remains virtually uncommercialised, a real part of Spain.

One of the notable axioms of Jerez applies, with a vengeance, during the sherry harvest festival. Sherry there is traditionally served in a tapered glass called a copita. You must, they say, have 'one before eleven, or eleven before one.' They mean eleven in the morning—and they are perfectly serious.

Montilla-Moriles

Montilla, sitting on a hilltop, is a typically Andalucian town. The cobbled streets are lined with orange trees. The houses of its people are whitewashed, neat, and set off by pots of geraniums bursting with colour. The homes of the wealthier Montillans are built around a courtyard where a tinkling fountain sends its cooling message. The small, palm-shaded parks are meeting places where the people can sit and talk, protected from the relentless summer sun.

Around Montilla, the rolling hills are a patchwork of olive groves, wheatfields and vineyards, a vista unchanged since the Romans first came to this region. It was here that the armies of

Julius Caesar finally put an end to the challenge from Pompey when they defeated an army led by Pompey's sons.

Montilla, and the neighbouring but now unimportant village of Moriles, have given their names to the denominacion of origin Montilla-Moriles. The wines of Montilla have been known and enjoyed for centuries, but it is only since the denominacion was created at the end of the Second World War that they have really come to stand in their own right.

The misfortune of Montilla was and still is that its wines are very similar to those of Jerez. So while they were known and enjoyed as Montilla wine in the region, in the bars of Cordoba with its startlingly beautiful old mosque, and in those of Madrid, they were little known elsewhere. The Jerezanos bought Montilla wine in substantial quantities, and while it entered their bodegas as Montilla, it emerged as sherry. Many an Englishman enjoying his glass of fino in the past would have been unaware that it could, wholly or in part, have been a Montilla fino. This may have been sharp practice, but in those days it was not illegal.

Since denominacion in 1944, it is, with one exception. So the Montilla producers have had to carve their own identity, and though overshadowed by sherry in both volume and reputation, it is to their credit that Montilla is now known and respected in its own right, both domestically and in other countries.

The vineyard area covers just under 16,000 hectares around 17 municipalities in the province of Cordoba, including Montilla and Moriles. The best soil for the grapes is the arctic white *albariza* of Jerez, which here can take on a greyish or pinkish tinge. These chalky soils are mainly found on the crests and slopes of the hills around Montilla, hills that have been graced with the name Sierra de Montilla, though it would take a fit person barely more than ten minutes to get to the top of one. These soils have been designated 'superior' for the production of Montilla wine, though they only account for about a fifth of the total area planted.

The other soil is called *ruedo*, and is either a brick red with a high iron content, or a grey clay. It is found in the lower lands around Montilla, and the flatter part of the denominacion away from the Sierra.

The first important difference between sherry and Montilla wine is the grape variety used to make each. In Jerez it is the Palomino, in Montilla the Pedro Ximinez, which is only used in Jerez to make a sweetening wine. In Montilla, the Pedro Ximinez accounts for 95 per cent of all plantings, the balance being Lairen [the Airen of La Mancha], Baladi, Torrontes and Moscatel.

125

They are lower trained than in Jerez, bush vines designed to preserve as much moisture as possible and protect the grapes from the sun. In the albariza soils they are permitted to yield up to 60 hectolitres per hectare, in ruedo soils up to 80 hectolitres.

When the grapes are picked they are taken to the bodegas and pressed. The best, like Alvear, use modern Willmes presses to extract juice gently, but most bodegas still use the chain press. Then the wine goes for its first fermentation. Today this is done in temperature-controlled stainless steel or resin-lined concrete tanks, but not so long ago it took place in the amphora-shaped tinajas. These tinajas still have an important part to play in the making of Montilla.

After the first fermentation, which lasts between five and seven days, the new wine is clarified and then transferred to tinajas for the second fermentation. These jars, which can hold anything between 3,000 and 10,000 litres, are never seen in Jerez, but are all over Montilla. They make a curiously splendid sight with their pointed bottoms propped up on the bodega floor. To work them, the bodegas have wooden slatted floors about two to three feet below the mouths of the tinajas, and when you stand on these slatted floors and look at the truncated tops of the tinajas in their neat rows, it is rather like seeing an array of very large breasts with commensurately large nipples. As there are plenty of second hand tinajas available, they are no longer made, but people still remember how to do so.

Once the second fermentation has finished in the tinajas, the wine is transferred to clean tinajas and the first flor starts to develop on its surface. Here it takes a variety of colours, bluish grey, off-white and various shades of green, giving a marbled paper effect on the surface of the wine. But because of the relative area of the flor skin to the amount of wine in the tinaja, it imparts little flavour to the wine.

While it is in the tinajas, the wine is classified. The two basic types of Montilla are fino and oloroso, just as in Jerez. The classification is done by aroma and taste by the bodega *capataz* [winemaster] and by laboratory analysis, and the two opinions, sensory and scientific, must concur.

There are no fixed rules, but in general the fino wine will come from free run and first pressing [*vino de yema*] juice from the superior albariza soils in the Sierra, while oloroso wine, fuller in body and higher in alcohol, will come from second pressing [*mosto color*] wines, usually from those grapes grown in the inferior ruedo soils and the flatter vineyards. Two other classifications sometimes made are raya, a wine near to but not quite an oloroso, and palo cortado, halfway between the two main styles.

The wine can stay in tinajas up to the end of June after the harvest, but it is progresively taken into the bodegas to undergo its maturation cycle.

Here there are two important differences between Jerez and Montilla. In Jerez all sherries are fortified to a greater or lesser degree, according to style, and all are flor affected, with generally the finos developing more flor, the olorosos less so, which determines *their* classification to a large extent.

In Montilla the finos are *never* fortified, but are left at their natural strength, ideally between 14 and 14.5 degrees alcohol. The Montillan producers will emphasise time and time again that their finos are natural wines. The olorosos may be fortified, but it depends on what alcohol degree they attained naturally, and in some harvests no fortification is needed.

Both Montillan styles will go into a solera system, but only the finos are allowed to develop flor. The olorosos are put into casks that are totally filled, so there is no room for the flor to grow, and are left to acquire their flavour partly through oxidation, and partly through exposure to older wines in the solera system.

A Montillan fino goes into standard *botas* [butts] filled up to two-thirds of their capacity, stacked in the cool, high-ceilinged traditional bodegas that are very similar to those of Jerez. The white flor skin develops on the surface of the wine, imparting its distinctive taste as the flor grows and then dies. Interestingly, it sometimes develops a double skin, one on the surface of the wine, one just above it.

When the flor has done its job, the wine goes into the solera system, based as it is in Jerez on criaderas supporting the main solera. In Jerez a row of butts is generally a criadera or solera. In Montilla a row of butts will be both criadera and solera, with the youngest criadera the top row of butts, and the solera at the bottom. The name solera comes from the Spanish word *suelo* which means ground, and the Montillans maintain that the best wine should be closest to the ground.

In Montilla, both finos and olorosos have to be in wood at least a year, but the good quality finos will be in the solera for two to three years, and the top quality ones a little longer.

In the case of an oloroso, the butt is filled to its capacity and stored either directly in the sun, as at Perez Barquero, or outside

A Montilla bodega, typically bedecked with flowers.

the bodega but partly covered, as at Alvear or Carbonell. The wine acquires its flavour through the combination of oxidation and the contact with older wine. Finally the wine is drawn off from the solera, with a maximum of 40 per cent of the content of the solera allowed to be taken off in any one year, and goes for bottling.

Within the basic framework of fino and oloroso, the Montillans make a variety of styles, just as the Jerezanos do. Here it is worth noting that the Montillans use the same names, fino, oloroso and so on, to describe the style of wine, except in the United Kingdom, where, after a lengthy court case brought by the sherry producers, the Montillans were ordered not to use such terms, and instead describe their fino as Pale Dry Montilla, for example.

A typical Montilla fino [pale dry] has a slightly pungent, somewhat tangy aroma, sometimes a touch fruity, and with a dry to slightly grapey flavour, quite savoury but not as crackingly bone dry as a Jerez fino.

When the fino is kept in its cask longer than its allotted time it develops into an amontillado [medium] Montilla. It annoys the

Montillans that the name itself derives from the Jerez saying, 'in the style of Montilla', and yet the Jerezanos have been granted legal protection for the name in Britain, when it is clear that in the past they were saying their wine was like that of Montilla, possibly suggesting that the Montilla was better.

A modern Montilla amontillado now only has a vague resemblance to that of Jerez, with a nutty colour, a light, slightly sweet aroma that can be fruity, have a touch of nuttiness, and sometimes a suggestion of raisins, and a flavour that ranges from softly fruity to quite dry.

However at Carbonell I was offered a glass of amontillado that had been in cask for 100 years, a beautiful wine with a deep orange gold colour, a superb soft, nutty, subtle aroma, and a penetratingly bone dry flavour, deliciously tangy and savoury, with a long, dry, mouthwatering aftertaste. One could see what the Jerezanos were getting at.

Pale cream montilla is a fino sweetened with concentrated grape must. A typical one is a honey yellow colour, with a soft, grapey sweet but clean aroma, and a grapey sweet flavour, not at all cloying, that leaves a slight sweetness in the mouth.

Oloroso seco is, as the name implies, oloroso straight from the solera. It will have a nut brown colour, a dryish, full, raisiny aroma, and a dry to very dry flavour with a touch of grapiness in the middle, and a dry tangy finish.

When an oloroso is sweetened with some concentrated Pedro Ximinez wine, it becomes a Montilla cream. To make the sweetening wine, the grapes are picked late and left out in the sun on grass mats for about two weeks. The grapes shrivel into raisins, and with hard pressing whatever juice remains is extracted. It is then vinified and passes through its own solera system.

There is a quite considerable production of this sweetening wine in Montilla, because it is the only wine that can still be legally sold to, and used by, Jerez, where it is utilised to make the sweet sherries by blending. Some Montilla bodegas produce only this wine, to supply the buyers from Jerez.

A Montilla cream will usually have a deep mahogany colour, a full but soft and raisiny aroma, sometimes with a slight burnt touch, and a full, soft, somewhat raisiny flavour, but finishing quite clean to leave a lingering sweetness in the mouth.

Finally there is limited bottling of Pedro Ximinez, in its concentrated form. It is such an intensely raisiny wine, both of aroma and flavour, so concentrated that it is difficult to drink. The Montillans like to pour a little over their dessert, be it ice cream or strawberries, but in some northern markets it is drunk as a dessert wine.

The Montillans would disagree with me, naturally, and they have every right to do so, but I find their Pedro Ximinez based Montillan sherries generally lack the finesse of the Palomino based sherries of Jerez, which at the drier end of the range are more penetratingly dry and have more style about them. There is certainly nothing in Montilla to compare with a classic Manzanilla.

However the bodegas themselves are just as attractive as those in Jerez, with high arched pillars supporting vaulted roofs, and compact earth floors that can be watered in the summer to keep temperatures down and humidities up.

The main exporting bodegas have banded themselves into an organization known as Montisierra. The oldest and largest member is Alvear, founded in 1729 in the centre of Montilla, and still owned by the same family. Its whitewashed bodega in the centre, ablaze in the summer with geraniums and clematis, and shaded by old palms, is supported by a second bodega, Las Puentes, in the superior zone. Alvear's main wines are CB Fino, and its top quality Festival Fino.

Carbonell, owned by an olive oil producing company, is based in Aguilar de la Frontera, the village that has taken over from Moriles as the second most important to Montilla. The Carbonell bodega is certainly the most beautiful in the region. It looks a century old, but is one of the newest, and no expense was spared in building it in the Andalucian style. Its main bodega is modelled on the Mosque of Cordoba, and matches anything seen in Jerez. The main Carbonell wine is Solera Fino.

The third main bodega is Perez Barquero, a former family firm that was bought by the Rumasa group, which spent considerable sums on modernising the bodega, and which is now owned by three local businessmen. Its leading wines are Barquero and Los Amigos finos, Los Palcos Amontillado and Diogenes Oloroso. The company also owns the Compania Vinicola del Sur, which produces the Monte Cristo range of Montillas.

Other bodegas include Montulia, Crismona, Navarro, Mora Chacon, Luque, Gracia and Garcia, and the co-operatives [which are not strong in this region] of Jesus Nazareno, Senora de la Aurora and La Purisma.

Four companies have also used their stainless steel equipment to produce light table wines, and it is interesting that the Pedro Ximinez seems to do better here than the Palomino in Jerez. The best are the lightly fruity Marques de la Sierra of Alvear, and the slightly drier, lemony Vina Amalia of Perez Barquero. The rather hard Vina Lairen of Crismona and the semi-sweet Vina Verde of Gracia are not so acceptable.

Within Spain, it is the finos that Montilla is known for, and despite stiff opposition from Jerez, Alvear's CB is the third largest selling fino-style wine. However, abroad it is the amontillado types that sell best, so there is a nice balance for the Montillans. Life has not always been that easy for them, and three bodegas, Cobos, Montialbero and Cruz Conde have closed down. However, those that remain have successfully made new wines out of some of the oldest wines of Spain.

Malaga

Malaga is one of the three 'Ms' of the fortified world that look back on a golden past, and forward to an uncertain future. Malaga has fallen from grace, marsala has been largely reduced to a wine used in sauces, and only madeira has pulled itself together and is building a better future.

Malaga's misfortune is to be a sweet liquorous wine, fortified with spirit, in a world where such wines, with the exception of port, madeira, and local specialities like the Australian muscat wines, are no longer what the average drinker wants. And part of the vineyard area is in a region where the pressure is on to use land for building.

The charming old town of Malaga on the south-east coast of Spain is the gateway to the Costa del Sol, beloved of the package holiday tourist hoping to escape the cold northern winter. Few would probably venture into Malaga with its wide, palm-lined streets, old Moorish Spanish homes, colourful Mediterranean gardens, cool and ablaze with bougainvillaeas and other flowers. The tourists leave the airport, skirt Malaga, and head for the architectural blight of the holiday hotels from Torremolinos to Marbella, and the raucous blight of the accompanying bars and discos. It is about as Spanish as steak and kidney pie.

Few of these tourists will ever taste malaga wine. They prefer beer and sangria. So even a local market has been denied to the

131

producers. Sales have been falling away, and urban encroachment, with consequent rising land values, are seeing the coastal vineyards being ripped out.

Malaga's decline is a pity, for as a wine it has a long and distinguished history. The vineyards were first planted by Greeks and Phoenicians, and were some of the first in Spain. *Malaka* was one of the earliest colonies of the Phoenician traders from north Africa. During the long period of Moorish domination, the vineyards flourished and expanded, despite the Koranic laws that saw most of the other vineyards in Spain disappear. One chronicler records in 1047 that Idriss II enjoyed the very sweet malaga wine called *Xarab al Malaqui,* or Malaga syrup, which is how the laws of the Koran were avoided.

After the reconquest the Catholic kings created a Brotherhood of Winegrowers in Malaga in 1487, a brotherhood which still exists today, and gave them a Royal Charter in 1502. Later Catherine the Great of Russia was a lover of malaga, but its golden days were in the 1800s when both America and Great Britain imported vast quantities of malaga wine. In the United Kingdom it was an important tipple for the ladies, known as Mountain, and was even more popular than sherry.

Then disaster struck. In 1876 phylloxera hit the Malaga vineyards, the first part of Spain to be hit by the louse. A total of 60,000 hectares of vines were killed off, more than 10,000 peasant families were ruined, and most were forced to emigrate to South America and take labouring jobs. It was a body blow from which Malaga never recovered. And when replanting did begin, the traditional export markets had lost the taste for malaga wine.

Today the Malaga region has 16,000 hectares of vineyards, of which only 3,000 are for making wine, the rest providing table grapes and raisins. It is broadly divided into two: the Axarquia in the south-eastern part around Malaga, Borge, Velez, Torrox and Competa, and the Antequera plateau in the north-west.

If Malaga's decline has had any beneficial effect it is the realisation that the coastal region, the flat strip alongside the rugged hills of Axarquia, and the pocket-sized vineyards in those hills, hence the Victorian name 'mountain wines', are not particularly suited to grape-growing for winemaking. The coastal vineyards are going to the property developers, and the hilly ones, extremely difficult to work, to table grapes.

However Axarquia, with its mild Mediterranean climate and slaty, sandy soils, is still important to the production of malaga wine, for it is where the Moscatel grape does best.

The rolling slopes of the Antequera plateau, rising to 500 metres above sea level, with its limestone soils, long, cold winters and short hot summers, and more easily worked terrain, allowing the use of mechanical equipment, is emerging as the favoured area, if at the moment it remains the smaller of the two.

It is where the Pedro Ximen or Pedro Ximinez does best. Interestingly, the name is attributed to the Flemish or German born Peter Simon, who saw some geographical resemblance to the Rhine and imported cuttings from Germany to plant in the Antequera.

Both grapes are now the cornerstone of malaga wine, and whereas in the past more than 30 varieties were planted in the region, these are now the only two that can be replanted, though small amounts of Lairen [Airen] and two others are also grown for specific purposes within the making of malaga.

The grapes are picked when fully ripe and taken to wineries near the vineyards. In days past, and even to some extent today, the poor roads and difficult terrain would have made it impossible to take the grapes to wineries in Malaga without some deterioration and oxidation, so all crushing and fermentation is done *in situ*.

Fermentation is traditionally done in oak casks or the curious cement or clay *tinajas* found in other parts of Spain, rather like large amphorae. However, a few progressive wineries have moved to temperature-controlled stainless steel. The initial tumultuous fermentation lasts from three to five days, then a longer, slower fermentation takes place over the next three weeks or so.

Once the new wine is made, it is transported to Malaga, because by decree of the local Consejo Regulador, all wine to be called malaga must be 'bred' within the confines of the town. This is not some idealistic decision foisted on the producers. The extremes of climate in the better vineyard areas would be detrimental to the ageing of the wine, whereas the mild Mediterranean climate and the cooling influence of the sea make Malaga town a positively beneficial place to age the wines slowly.

The best producers retain some of their grapes up country and put them out in the sun on grass esparto mats for 15–20 days to shrivel and concentrate the juices before they are allowed to ferment. Some producers use drying chambers to achieve the same effect.

Four secondary 'wines' can also be made to be used in blending to achieve a certain style of malaga. In essence they are concentrates. Arrope is a syrup made by heating grape must to caramelise the sugar. Vino de Color is made in the same way, but the juice is almost reduced to a paste. Vino Tierno is made from sun-dried grapes allowed to ferment out to almost natural strength, while Vino Mastro is partly fortified before fermentation to give around 15 degrees of alcohol. All four are used for sweetening, colouring or strengthening.

Malaga is a blended wine, just as sherry or port are, but there are no hard and fast rules about when this is done. Some producers do it before maturation, others after, some according to style. However, maturation, usually in chestnut casks, is the key to malaga. The rules say the wine must be matured in cask for a minimum two years, but in practice it goes on much longer.

Some wines are simply held in casks for the required period, but the quality malagas pass through the same solera system as found in Jerez, a sort of vinous chain where fractions of wine pass up an age scale, taking on the characteristics of the older wines they meet till they are fully mature. If you applied the pyramid selling system to the making of malaga, the best position would be at the top of the triangle, while those below wait their turn, while feeding the chain.

Some very venerable soleras exist, going back to the last century. However, a wine lover finding an old malaga dating from, say, 1850, should not start rubbing his hands with glee at a 'discovery'. This date only indicates when the solera began, not the age of the wine.

Malaga is not just malaga. There are several distinct styles based on sweetness [dry, mild, semi dry, semi sweet] and colour [white, gold, golden red, dark and black].

Without question the blue-blooded aristocrat is Malaga Lagrima. It used to be made only from the juice oozing from bunches of grapes hung to dry. It would be out of the question to do this today. The wine would be far too expensive. So it is made from the juice that escapes the grapes by the sheer weight of those piled on top, and no juice from the presses is used.

The best lagrimas are deep golden tawny wines, made from the tears [lagrima] of the grapes, full bodied but smooth, with a slightly toasted character on the palate. Wines of rarity and finesse, they are some of the greatest to come out of Spain.

Malaga Moscatel from only that grape has a deep golden to amber colour, with a rich, aromatic, grapey aroma and flavour that varies from semi sweet to dry. It is a true dessert wine of which the poet Escovar wrote:

A girl, a guitar,
and a glass of Moscatel
in half an hour made
an Englishman become an Andalusian.

Its other half is Malaga Pedro Ximen. When fully mature it is a dark amber with reddish highlights, has an intense grapey aroma, and a full, smooth, slightly raisiny flavour with a bitter sweet finish.

Lesser-known styles include Pajarete, which borders on a black colour, but yet is the driest of traditional malagas, and the one best suited to drink as an aperitif. Dulce [sweet] color has some Arrope in it to give a dark amber colour and a rich and ripely grapey flavour. Malaga seco is made from Pedro Ximen fermented almost right out, giving a dryish wine, pale gold in colour, with a dryish aroma and dry tangy flavour. It is rarely seen outside the area, but offers an alternative to Pajarete.

Quite a few malagas carry some indication of age, but the old solera malagas are the ones that each bodega takes pride in, and *trasanejas* are ones that can go back to casks laid down more than two centuries ago. They have a lovely colour, amber or mahogany, sweet nutty aromas, and rich but dryish flavours complemented by raisiny middle palates. They are something quite special.

The best producers deserve an award for continuing to make wines in the face of every reason not to do so, and maintaining an historic Spanish tradition. Those with a well-deserved reputation for quality are Antonio Barcelo [Bacarles and Sanson labels], Larios, Montealegre, Casa de Guardia, La Manchega, Lopez Hermanos, and the best of them all, Scholtz Hermanos, whose Solera 1885 is the standard by which all malagas should be judged.

The average Malagan has an ad hoc attitude towards drinking malaga. He will take a glass or two whenever it takes his fancy. But in truth these are fine dessert wines and should be treated as such, with puddings, nuts or just as a fine drink after dinner. The late Harry Yoxall called them 'dark fires in the heart of a jewel'. Perhaps if more people took to malaga, one of Spain's most historic wines could enjoy a minor renaissance and become one of the new wave wines of Spain.

CHAPTER 11

Other Wines of Spain

The countries that rim the northern Mediterranean are blessed for the most part with an equitable climate, a climate that perfectly suits the vine. Provided the soil is fair, and sufficient water is available naturally or through irrigation, the warm sun will induce the vine to produce an abundance of grapes. The grower only has to tend his vineyard, watch out for pests, and harvest this abundance when the grapes are ripe.

Spain, of all the countries of the Mediterranean, has embraced this natural gift wholeheartedly. From the very north, along the rim of the Pyrenees, to the very south, looking out to Gibraltar, and across the sea to Majorca, Minorca and Ibiza, there is hardly an arable part of Spain where vines have not been planted. Every tiny village *cantina* will have its local wine. Grape-growing, wine-making and wine drinking is part of the Spanish way of life.

In most parts of Spain it is a cottage industry, just as it is in many parts of Italy or Greece, and to a lesser extent France. The farmer plants some vines as one of his crops, and either he or the local co-operative vinifies the grapes. Part of the wine is for his own table, some may go into large glass jars for sale in the local grocer's shop or through the village bar. The wine will rarely move outside his own community.

Wine consumption in Spain is the fifth highest in the world, but in common with Italy, the largest producer, and France, it is shrinking. Though the Spanish growers have embraced the co-operative movement with greater fervour than their neighbours, and even though Spain has more vines planted than anywhere else, the acreage is declining. The reason is a combination of farmers' sons leaving the land, farmers finding it more profitable to plant other crops and buy their wine ready-made from producers who show economies of scale, and the increasing sophistication of the average Spanish wine drinker.

An increasing realisation that wine too is a commodity is seeing the decline of the peasant grower and the rise of the bigger co-operatives and private bodegas.

So the seeker after Spanish wine should turn this way. To be sure there is always the tourist who 'discovers' the local wine, enthuses about it when back home, and wonders why he cannot find it in his local bottle shop. The answer is that the authorities would probably ban it from export for various reasons.

Spain has 30 denominaciones of origin, those areas supposedly singled out as producing the best wines, though this is not always necessarily the case. Well-organised groups of farmers can exert considerable political pressure to get what they want—not only in Spain. This criticism has been regularly levelled at the Italians. More denominaciones are in the pipeline, and with Spain's accession to the European Community, with its various rules and regulations governing wine quality, it is an advantage to have a denominacion.

Most of the existing denominaciones have all been covered to a greater or lesser extent in earlier chapters. This chapter deals in broad outline with some of the other wines to be found in Spain that are local in origin, nature and consumption, but about which the author will be accused of ignorance by the wine-drinking tourist who happens to read this book, if something is not said about them.

Generally my recommendation is to stick to the better-known wines in bottle from the better-known regions. They will usually be available outside their own provinces. But there is always the possibility of discovering an interesting 'local' wine.

The traveller crossing from France into Spain and continuing to follow the coast through San Sebastian and Bilbao, comes to Santander, on the Atlantic coast. Once a minor seat of Royal power, it is now better known as a holiday resort, and one of the homes of Spanish yachtsmen.

Outside Santander there was once a flourishing wine industry, but it has now virtually disappeared. However, the wine lover with a penchant for hunting down obscure local wines may come across a very light, somewhat acidic white wine made from the Zuria or Tzuri grape. It has a distant kinship to the needle wines of Galicia, further along the coast.

One wine that can still be found in tiny quantities in the Basque country is txacoli or chacoli, which comes from 37 hectares of vines around Guetaria. Chacoli is made locally from the red Hondarrubibeltza and white Hondarrubizuri grapes, though imported wine is also used. Mostly it is a white, light, delicate, slightly petillant wine, quite acidic, and similar in style to the white wine of Galicia. A red version can also be found.

Two bodegas produce chacoli commercially, the best known being Txomin Etxaniz, the other Eizaguirre.

Toro, to the west of the denominacion Rueda, is Spain's newest denominacion and its wines can be found in the bars of Zamora and the old world town of Toro.

The vineyards, planted in the near flat valley of the river Duero with its dry climate, have a long and proud history. Toro wines were enjoyed by kings and commoners as far back as the twelfth century, and were considered of such value that when the famous Cathedral of Santiago de Compostella was given a Toro vineyard by King Alfonso IX in 1208, it was a red-letter day for the monks.

Less than 100 years ago, Toro was exporting considerable amounts of wine to other parts of Spain, but phylloxera, severe drought at the end of the last war, and declining sales, saw many of the historic vineyards torn out and replaced with wheat.

The white Albilla wine has virtually disappeared, but the red Tinto de toro, from Tinto de Toro, Tinto de Madrid and Garnacha grapes, is still made, though most of it is sold in bulk.

It is a very deep and powerful wine, heady to say the least, strong in colour, high in alcohol, but low in acidity, so the wine smooths out rather quickly. Jan Read, in *The Wines of Spain*, observes: 'It has been said that the wine of Toro is not for drinking, not even for eating, but devouring; and though pure gold, it is as black as a Moor.'

Certainly Toro has a strong affinity with the better known Priorato of Tarragona.

Examples can be found in bottle from Villar, Luis Mateos, Vinedos Morales, the Cooperativa de Morales and Porto. In Zamora the better known Bodegas Otero produces a red and white Vina Alegré.

To the north of nearby Valladolid is another historic wine-producing area, but with more of a future. Cigales is overshadowed by its neighbours Rueda and Ribera del Duero, but it combines something of each in that it produces both red and white wines, and has the varieties of both these other two denominaciones planted.

The area under vine in Cigales is actually increasing slightly, but again most of it is sold for blending or as bulk wine, and not much is bottled. It is readily available in Valladolid, where it has been sold for several centuries, but only the better restaurants would have it in bottle.

Extraordinarily, much of the wine made by the locals is still made in the typical Castillian cellars of the past, underground bodegas that have not seen a whiff of modern winemaking techniques, and are much the same as they were in the thirteenth century. The white wines and rosés made are undistinguished. It is the red Cigales that is worth looking for. It can be made from Garnacha, Tinto del Pais and Tinto de Madrid grapes, but the producers traditionally include some juice from the white Verdejo or Albillo grapes. The result is a bright cherry-coloured wine with a fresh, aromatic bouquet and a light but smooth and attractive flavour.

Not all Cigales is what it purports to be, but a first-class example is the wine produced by Vincente Conde Camazon, and other good examples come from Manuela Mantecon, Rodriguez Sanz and Pablo Barrigon Tovar.

A little further north again, and also serving the bars of Burgos, is La Ribera de Burgos, supposedly heading for denominacion status, though at the moment only two local co-operatives, Roa and La Horra, sell wine in bottle. Two styles of red wine are made, primarily from Tinto del Pais grapes, a lighter, fresher, younger and fruitier wine, and a fuller, deeper, more alcoholic one. Before the advent of the Spanish wine laws, quite a lot of Ribera de Burgos wine disappeared into the Rioja, but now it has shrunk back to the status of local house wine, of minor interest to the traveller visiting the splendid cathedral of Burgos.

An appendage to the southern part of Navarra, and overshadowed by Navarra and Rioja, is the minor denominacion Campo de Borja in the province of Zaragoza. The highish vineyards are planted mainly with Garnacha for red and rosé wines, with a little Bobal and Vidadico and a tiny amount of Macabeo for white or blending wine.

The area is dominated by co-operatives, Santo Cristo, Nino

Perdido, Borja and Juan Bautista. The only private producer to bottle wine is Angel Bordeje.

The principal wine of the denominacion is a deep to very deep, high in alcohol, dry and full-bodied red wine with a characteristic bitter twist at the finish. It is a good blending wine, so that is where much of it goes. What is bottled should be treated with cautious respect.

A little further south is the more thrusting new denominacion Carinena, which gave its name to the grape variety, though carinena as a variety has virtually disappeared from Carinena as a denominacion.

Carinena is south of Zaragoza in the highest Aragon hinterland, though the climate is dry and the rainfall low. These conditions would naturally yield full-bodied red wines, and that, for centuries, was the reputation of Carinena in Madrid and Barcelona. They were, and still are, also excellent wines for blending. However, some bodegas are also moving with the times and making a lighter clarete style of red wine.

The principal grape is the Garnacha, which forms the basis of almost all the red wines made, and some Viura is also grown for blending or bottled white wine.

The typical Carinena tinto is full-bodied, robust, with plenty of alcohol, good tannins and needs some time in bottle to round off. There should be a touch of violets on the nose. The clarete wines are lighter, fruitier and fresher, softer and ready to drink when bottled. The denominacion also has a tradition of making *rancio* wines, and the white table wines known as *pajarillas*, mainly for local consumption.

Quite a few bodegas are producing respectable wine, with Vicente Suso the best, and the private producers Lacosta, Tejero, Martinez Gutierrez, Joaquin Soria, Palafox, and the co-operatives San Valero, Aguila, Carinena and San José all worth trying.

Carinena may not have done enough to make people really sit up and take notice, but it is a denominacion to watch.

Elsewhere in Aragon, Somontano in the north, lying in the foothills of the Pyrenees, has recently been granted denominacion status, and is making some attractively light, soft and fruity red wines, while aspirants Calatayud, which is extensively planted, is yielding dry day-to-day reds, and Valdejalon offers deeper, fuller-bodied dry and somewhat lean reds.

In the Tarragon hinterland, high in plateau country, is the area known as Conca de Barbera, the only major Tarragona vineyard area without denominacion, though it is provisionally listed.

When it is virtually impossible to find a Conca wine in bottle, this listing seems rather premature.

The cool climate produces delicate wines from the same varieties as are planted in the Penedes, and almost all the white wine made goes straight to the cellars of the Cava producers, while the rosés and reds find their way to other bodegas where they lose their identity.

Perhaps those bodegas know they are onto a good thing, and prefer to leave matters as they are. However, this beautiful, mountainous, rarely visited part of northern Spain may one day become a source of some excellent wines.

Mentrida is the closest denominacion to Madrid, lying just south of the Spanish capital in the province of Toledo. Yet despite its proximity to the biggest market in the country, the wines of Mentrida are relatively unknown outside the region, and only a small percentage of the total production is available in bottle.

The basic Mentrida wine is a deep purply red wine, fat, strong in alcohol, and robustly dry, made from Garnacha grapes, which are also used to make some local rosés. It is a decent wine for blending or selling in bulk to the local restaurants and bars. Among the few who bottle Mentrida wine are the bodegas La Cerca and Valdeoro, and the co-operative Campo San Roque.

Just to the west, in the lee of the Sierra de Gredos, a popular summer retreat for the citizens of Madrid, is the area called Cebreros, which despite its location has a more Mediterranean type climate, due to the higher altitudes of the vineyards and the extra rainfall they receive.

The grapes grown are Garnacha, Albillo and Aragones, which are used to produce both clarete and tinto red wines. Both usually have an alcohol degree in excess of 13, which gives the claretes a very dry, almost astringent character. The tintos, despite being full and dry, are softer and smoother due to the local habit of adding a little white grape juice from the Albillo to the cepage.

The Cebreros tintos have long been popular in Madrid, which is why the region has some chance of achieving denominacion, but within the Spanish context they are rather undistinguished. Bodegas Perlado and the Grupo Sindical de Colonizacion No 795 [the latter an interesting name to put on a label as it sounds more like a lottery] both sell wine in bottle.

Sandwiched between Mentrida and Cebreros is the grouping of three small wine regions known collectively as the Tierra de Madrid. As with Cebreros, it is an area known for strong red wine from the Garnacha grape, softened with some white Albillo juice, and these wines too have long stood on the tables of Madrid, even in the Royal Palace. They have a loyal following in the capital, but are not much seen elsewhere.

Again most of the wine from Tierra de Madrid is sold in bulk, but one producer, Bodegas Hijos de Jesus Diaz, won a major award in a domestic wine-tasting by a respected wine club, much to the surprise of many, and subsequently has become one of the 'discovered' wines of Spain. The Arganda co-operative and the private producer Ricardo Benito also sell wine in bottle.

Extremadura is the province that abuts the southern border with Portugal. Mountainous, hard country, with its highest hills timbered with oak and chestnuts, it is by and large home only to lonely shepherds and their wandering flocks.

It is a sparsely populated, less than prosperous part of Spain that traditionally sent its hardiest men abroad to find fame and fortune, men like Pizarro, the son of a swineherd, who conquered the Incas, and Cortez, who found his fame in Mexico.

Within this ruggedly beautiful land, famous for its 'viper-fed' hams, made, according to the traveller Richard Ford, from pigs that feasted on the vipers that infested the Sierra de las Viboras, are fertile valleys where fig, cherry and olive trees are interspersed with vineyards producing wine mainly for local consumption.

In the Caceres region, the valley of Jerte produces a lightish red wine with a characteristic bitterness, but it is the wine from Montanchez and five other nearby villages that is perhaps the best known of the region. A white wine is made from Borba, Pedro Ximinez and Cayetana grapes, and a red from Garnacha, Bejen and Monastrell. What makes these wines unique is that the new wine is put into earthenware *tinajas* [large jars], only partly filled, and left over the next 12 months to develop a flor scum on the surface that increases the alcohol content of the wine up to around 14.5 degrees, and imparts a taste akin to the sherries of Jerez and the flor wines of Montilla.

The white wine takes on an orange hue and has more of the scent of a sherry, while the red wine is quite full-bodied with less flor character. Both have a distinguishing earthy taste. The co-operative of Montanchez is the main producer, while the private bodegas Galan y Berrocal and Rosco both bottle the local wine. Nearby Canamero also produces flor wines that have a following, and a little is seen in Madrid.

Canamero wine does, however, differ from those of Montanchez in that both red and white wines are mixed together and then the flor is allowed to develop on the combined juice. Bodegas

Ruiz is the only one to bottle this wine. The intrepid visitor may also taste a wine called *de pitarra*, which is made by a crude form of *maceracion carbonique* in that the grapes, including the skins, are sealed in jars and allowed to ferment. After some time the seal of the jar is pierced to allow the carbon dioxide to escape, and then the wine is allowed to settle before it is drunk.

The Extremaduran province of Badajoz produces much more wine, and of a conventional nature. The main producing region is the flattish Tierra de Barros, where the vineyards are planted in muddy soils that once formed the basis of a pottery industry. In winter the soils are thick mud, while the dry summers send yields shooting up.

The main local wine is made from the white grape Cayetana Blanca, which yields a light, dry, neutral wine, low in alcohol, that has a tendency to maderise quickly. Much of it is sent for distillation into brandy, for which it is ideally suited, and the brandy then goes south to fortify the sherries of Jerez. Some better examples of these wines come from Cevisur, Antonio Sanchez and, elsewhere in the region, from Garcia Avila, Zaymar and Ortega.

The denominacion of origin of Huelva runs from the river Guadalquivir west towards the Portuguese border in the very south of Spain. In Palos, on the coast near the town of Huelva, a statue commemorates the last Spanish landfall of Christopher Colombus before he sailed to find the New World, and the vineyard region adjoins the famous Marismas bird sanctuary.

Except for the widespread planting of the white Zalema grape variety, the Huelvan wines are pretty much identical to those of Jerez, but without the quality, and are made in the same way.

The lighter Palidos wines are roughly equivalent to a fino, the Soleras wines to an amontillado, and Ambarsto to olorosos. Some fairly full-bodied white wines are also made. Amongst the producers who bottle these *generosos* are the bodegas Andrade, Francisco Vallejo, Juan Perea, Miguel Salas and Raposo.

The sun-drenched Balearic islands, Majorca, Minorca and Ibiza, attract thousands of tourists every year, and some will drink the local wines made for centuries on Majorca. Cyrus Redding in his classic *The History and Description of Modern Wines*, published in 1833, noted that Majorca produced a rather good red wine called Aleyor, but added: 'the white wines are made in a slovenly way, somewhat in the mode adopted in Cyprus, which would seem to indicate that the art had been brought there first, and not acquired from Spain.'

Today the main Majorcan vineyards are around Binisalem in the centre of the island and Felanitx in the south-east. The main varieties grown are the little-known Manto Negro, Callet and Fogoneu. The Manto Negro yields a full-bodied, somewhat coarse red wine, the Fogoneu a softish local rosé. The private producer Jose L. Ferrer makes the best wines on the island, a fresh, young red, and deeper, fuller reserva red, which are worth looking for.

The Canary Islands had their vinous heyday in the times of William Shakespeare, who mentioned Canary wine in several of his plays, including Henry IV, Part Two, where Mistress Quickly says: 'But i'faith, you have drunk too much canaries, and that's a marvellous searching wine, and it perfumes the blood ere one can say, What's this?'

A couple of centuries later, Cyrus Redding was equally complimentary: 'Canary was once drunk much in England, and was known only by that name. The writer of this tasted some which was a hundred and twenty-six years old, it having been kept during all that period in the family cellars of a nobleman, with whom he happened to be dining, and who produced the bottle as a bon bouche. Its flavour was good, and it had ample body.'

Redding goes on to say that a lot of Canary wine was mistaken for, or substituted for madeira, with which it had a strong likeness. Today wine is still made on the Canary Islands, but it is now only a shadow of its former self.

The mountainous volcanic nature of Tenerife, Las Palmas and Lanzarote mean that most of the Canary vineyards are small, hard to work plots of vines, scattered throughout the islands.

The black Listan grape produces a heady, robust red wine, and the white Listan a full bodied, perfumed dry white wine. But the best Canary wines, which hark back to the days of old, come from the Malvasia grape, full-bodied wines that border on being dessert wines in style, amber coloured and sweet. Those of Bodegas Mozaga and El Grifo on Lanzarote and Teneguia on Las Palmas are the ones to look for in this, the furthest outpost of Spanish viticulture.

BIBLIOGRAPHY

Club de Gourmet, *Wines of Spain*, 1985/6 edition.

Decanter Magazine, various articles.

Fuentes, Adolfo Vasserot, *Malaga Wine*, Grupo Comercial Malaga, 1978.

Gonzalez Gordon, Manuel M., *Sherry The Noble Wine*, The Cookery Book Club, 1948.

Gourmetour Magazine, various articles.

Guia Practica de los Vinos de Espana, 1983.

Jeffs, Julian, *Sherry*, Faber & Faber, 1982.

Johnson, Hugh, *Wine*, Mitchell Beazley, 1974.

Johnson, Hugh, *Wine Companion*, Mitchell Beazley, 1983.

Johnson, Hugh, *World Atlas of Wine, Third Edition*, Mitchell Beazley, 1985.

Layton, T. A., *Wines and Castles of Spain*, Michael Joseph, 1959.

Penin, José, *Manual de Vinos Espanoles*, Penthalon, 1982.

Pohren, D. E., *Adventures in Taste, The Wines and Folk Food of Spain*, Society of Spanish Studies, 1972.

Rainbird, George, *Sherry and the Wines of Spain*, Michael Joseph, 1966.

Read, Jan, *The Wines of Spain*, Faber & Faber, 1982.

Read, Jan, *Wines of the Rioja*, Sotheby Publications, 1984.

Reay-Smith, John, *Discovering Spanish Wine*, Robert Hale, 1976.

Redding, Cyrus, *A History and Description of Modern Wines*, Whittaker, Treacher & Arnot, 1833.

Salter, Cedric, *Introducing Spain*, Methuen, 1953.

Simon, André, *Wine in Shakespeare's Days and Shakespeare's Plays*, The Curwen Press, 1964.

Sitwell, Sacheverell, *Spain*, B. T. Batsford, 1950.

Torres, Miguel A., *The Distinctive Wines of Catalonia*, Hymsa, 1986.

INDEX

146